THE NEW HUMANITY

A Movement to Change the World

RENNIE DAVIS

The New Humanity
Volume I: Our Roots

Published by BlissLife Press.

BlissLife Press
Las Vegas, NV
BlissLifePress.com

For ordering information or special discounts for bulk purchases, Please contact BlissLife Press at BlissLifePress.com

First Edition

ISBN: 978-0-9977392-6-8

Cover design by Gail Carey
Interior Book Design by BlissLife Press Team -Christopher Sherrod

We LOVE Trees! For every book published at BlissLife Press we plant one hundred or more Trees. We support Trees for the Future, planting Tree farms that produce food, shade, clean air and a sustainable income.

Manufactured in the United States of America
10 9 8 7 6 5 4 3 2 1

Every attempt has been made to properly source all quotes.

Disclaimer: The names, locations, and events described in this book are largely based on the author's experiences and recollections. Any inaccuracies or misstatements are his own.

Logo: For this trilogy of books, the phoenix is the image of a new humanity at the crossroads of evolution rising to inspire a new way of living on Earth.

Stay Connected. To follow the latest book updates and tour events; To learn more about The New Humanity movement

Visit these links

Free protest and movement guide:
www.newhumanitybook.com

Information and Inquiries:
Rennie@RennieDavis.com

FOR KIRSTEN

I missed you in the Sixties but cherish your passion and wisdom now.

ACKNOWLEDGMENTS

The New Humanity was conceived deep down inside the geological wonder of the Grand Canyon. This vision emerged while listening to the Earth. To write one sentence about every person who also contributed might need another book, however. With many contributors and supporters, the vision of a new humanity evolved into a trilogy of books, asking one question. Can the best of humanity transcend the drama and trauma of today's fear and division and change the world?

In recent years, I joined a conversation that was difficult and challenging. It entertained an unsettling proposition—that our current civilization is unsustainable and humanity is in trouble. For society, the idea seems silly. Most people find it hard to imagine a great seismic shift coming to our present time. This trilogy emerged from this difficult conversation—one that is spreading by leaps and bounds as people figure it out and want to do something about the staggering challenge that is coming our way.

For this first book, I returned to the Sixties to glean and distill the lessons and insights that are relevant again today. For this first book, I had the advantage of many contributors and Alan Wartes was among them. I was fortunate to have had his support at the beginning. He encouraged me to share my Sixties stories when I was riveted on civilization's unsustainable trajectory. Recalling the magic of the Sixties[1] for its relevance again today, this first volume—*Our Roots*—returns to the Sixties to understand how we did it then so today's movement to change the world is better prepared and effective.

The Roots of today's movement is the Sixties and that earlier movement is rich with experiences that have value again. That's why I decided to organize a collection of some of the "greatest Sixties stories ever" into one volume for a new generation today. I want to thank the people who contributed their stories but also

1 For the purposes of this book, the term "Sixties" is used to refer to the movement, while '60s refers solely to the decade.

acknowledge the assistance of Wikipedia that kept me straight with dates, fact-checks, and spelling of names.

TheLea Brooks is a friend who seems to feel every subtle energy enveloping the world. She sensed what I was up to and with her husband Philip gave me a quiet space to work. David Christner who is pioneering one of the significant healing discoveries of our time supported me to write. Randall Prouty shared his new way of building for the time that is coming. Brilliant inventors also joined in with breakthrough technologies that convinced me that a local community can disconnect from an unsustainable global economy and live and thrive without hardship and struggle. Step by step, a design for how we could live on Earth without destroying the planet emerged like a barn-raising with many helping hands.

Along with Alan Wartes who came at the beginning, my invaluable other editor was Tyler Tichelaar who came at the end. Lois and Douglas Chambers corrected the typos with a final edit.

When it came time to publish this book, Ken Rush, David Christner, Eric Quade, Bill Spencer, Thomas Kaufmann and Mike Chang provided needed support. David Bellharz helped me empower the Agent Orange America Vietnam initiative that can be part of today's movement. Glennie Feinsmith helped me make the final push that launched this book.

My graphic artist friend Gail Carey inspired the book's cover design, and publishing coaches Nan Akasha and Chris Sherrod with their Bliss Life Press team including their marketing wizard Dale Thomas Vaughn got me on the road with copies of the book.

Many people had compelling Sixties experiences that created this collection of riveting stories including John Lennon and Yoko Ono, John Kerry, Tom Hayden, John Denver, Bobby Seale, Abbie Hoffman, Jerry Rubin, Dave Dellinger, John Lewis, Martin Luther King, Jr., Bob Moses, Julian Bond, Madam Nguyen Thi Binh, Neil Young, Ramsey Clarke and Roy Wilkins to name but a few. Mayor Richard Daley and Judge Julius Hoffman were some of the reluctant contributors to these Sixties lessons relevant for today.

Thanks also to Arthur K. Pope who sent me an email the day I began writing this book. He opened my eyes to my teenage years when I was mostly asleep to the troubles and blind spots of my high school white—only culture. Of course, sleepy normal places like rural Virginia where I grew up can become a springboard for revolutionaries who change the world—and I feel honored to be one of the many among them.

The New Humanity is my name for the global movement that is coming. At its roots, today's movement must become a journey to evolve ourselves. Ignited by the election of Donald J. Trump, events are coming that will push us off the fence to change how we live on Earth. My sense of the accelerating climate change timing comes from a science that is realizing harsh events are moving faster than previously forecasted.

When the Sixties revolution finally cooled down, our movement transitioned back to society. During the transition, many of us lived on farms and observed the intelligence of nature. We helped build the permaculture network that has become such a vital network for the time that is coming. As food insecurity turns more ominous, permaculture will be one of our cornerstones for feeding ourselves and the world. Gary Freeborg is one of the bright lights of the Permaculture revolution and he helped me realize the importance of mimicking the ways of the beavers (Volume II) and following the principles of nature during the time that is coming.

I want to thank David Fenton who made his Shots: *An American Photographer's Journal 1967-1972* available for this book. Thanks also to my sister Bea and her husband Mike Ponder too for finding some faded pictures of Morgan's Mill Farm and other early teenage memories.

Kirsten Liegmann is my wife and life partner. She wrote the *Foreward* that explains the mission of The New Humanity trilogy. You will find her insights and encouragement running throughout the trilogy, nourishing the reader who yearns to change the outcome of a challenging time.

When the Sixties Revolution ended, I began a search for practical options to the unsustainable practices threatening our planet. Today, I am one of millions of people who make up this extraordinary segment of the human race. The New Humanity is the largest constituency in history dedicated to creating a new paradigm on Earth. I especially want to thank you for finding your way to this book.

CONTENTS

FOREWORD

There is an age-old adage that says *timing is everything*!

Many works of art, words of wisdom and wondrous events have passed through history unnoticed and devoid of their unfulfilled potential. However, there have been moving words, inspiring visions and events, aligned to the energies of the time that truly did change the world. Martin Luther King's "I have a dream" blew a life-giving breath into the flames that were already licking at the edges of an entrenched, racially biased society. Similarly Mahatma Gandhi's call to "Be the change you wish to see in the world" was impeccably timed and continues to inspire an awakening humanity today.

Only a few books have ever had the precision of timing to shape the transition of an historic stage. Thomas Paine's *Common Sense* was an incendiary publication that came out at the beginning of the American Revolution. It spoke plainly about the issue on everyone's mind, making the case for freedom from British rule when the 13 colonies were still undecided. Thomas Paine called for an American Revolution with a prose people could understand. He connected his vision of independence with what people were feeling in their lives. *Common Sense*, as we know, changed the course of history.

I believe the Rennie Davis trilogy—the first book you are holding in your hand—has the potential to open the gateway for humanity to choose and create a different collective story as well.

I have had the honor of sharing my life with Rennie for a decade now. I have come to understand the lasting impact of his role at the eye of the societal hurricane that swept the United States in the 60s. I also know him for who he is today. Without a shadow of a doubt his greatest contribution is yet to come.

Born in 1968 and in Germany to boot, I had no clue who Rennie Davis was when we first met. What I remember most from that first encounter was the powerful presence of his eyes emanating a gentle yet urgent calm. During that evening event in Ashland,

Oregon, he spoke of his growing sense of a new, even more massive movement building beneath the surface of today's society – a quiet revolution that understood that fundamental change in the way human beings live on Earth was necessary to have a future.

Little by little, moved by his compelling storytelling and recollections of many other Sixties activists, I learned about the many world-changing events that shaped that era of U.S. history. Through persistence, courage and persuasive eloquence, Rennie helped inspire an entire generation to become one of the most powerful agents of change the world had ever seen.

The stories in this first book read like they came from some fantastical movie script. They are filled with suspense, heroism and humor, mixed with a dash of youthful recklessness. As the national coordinator of the largest coalition of anti-war and civil rights organizations in the late Sixties, Rennie organized many large protests coast to coast. From his own inside perspective he gives a behind-the-scenes account of these events, including the May Day protest that nearly shut down the federal government in Washington, D.C. and resulted in the largest arrest in American history. He recounts in vivid detail the day when 90% of all U.S. colleges and universities shut down from a nationwide student strike in response to the U.S. invasion of Cambodia. He takes you right into the middle of one of the most impactful events of that time that he co-directed with Tom Hayden, the demonstration against the war in Vietnam at the Democratic National Convention in Chicago -one that nearly cost Rennie his life. That event propelled him and seven other defendants into THE political trial of the 20th Century and turned the Chicago 7 into a legend of the Sixties. Rennie also partnered with John Lennon to bring a million people to the Republican National Convention. Some of his most precious memories of that time will take your breath away!

So, yes, this is an enormously entertaining story. And, yes, it is an important contribution to the annals of history. Far more important though is that Rennie never loses sight of the value of an impeccably timed clarion call to a new generation. The mission of this whole trilogy is to ask one burning question of all of us, right here, right now, living on Earth today and sensing that something is terribly amiss: "Are we just another generation passing through this world like all previous generations, or is this a time like no other?" Rennie Davis lays out with conviction and clarity that this is a time like no other—a time to come together again for a global movement more dramatic and impactful than the Renaissance, the American Revolution and the Sixties combined—a movement to change the human story and redefine our relationship to the Earth and each other.

Presented in three volumes—*(I) Our Roots; (II) Humanity at the Crossroads and (III) The Rise of Ilian— The New Humanity* trilogy appears at a juncture when the planet's climate is rapidly and dramatically shifting and many ecosystems are collapsing. Whether we are aware of it or not, challenges of unimaginable proportions are barreling toward us. While these three books do not promote the mindset of doom and gloom, they speak plainly about the issues many of us feel on a deep level. Humanity is in trouble and gridlocked governments seem unable to comprehend or respond to the changing reality around them. What Rennie presents is a refreshingly common sense description of what is truly happening in our world while making the case that there is something we can do about all the challenges that have been largely ignored.

Take, for example, the massive loss of biodiversity in one generation combined with the greatest extinction of species since the end of the dinosaurs. Contrary to public opinion, these two crises are not isolated events irrelevant to our city-led lives. They are panic alarms going off and screaming out that humanity is in trouble.

Since the beginning of the industrial revolution, civilization has spawned a vast global economy that is completely devoid of understanding that humanity is a wholly-owned subsidiary of a living whole system planet. The people driving our economy have never understood—or have ignored—that civilization, as it is currently designed, is unsustainable. Instead of rising to the occasion to change how we live on Earth, every nation has pledged their allegiance to unlimited growth and consumption without regard to the planet's resource trajectory. In fact, growth and consumption is considered the only economic model possible. As our global civilization barrels towards its inevitable collision with its own behavior, scientific reports that conclude our oceans are dying don't make the front page of our largest newspapers. Instead, the science that shows our atmosphere is more carbon polluted than any time in the past 15 million years is ignored or denied. Ignoring the reality that slash and burn is destroying our rainforests, civilization conveniently forgets that these vast "Earth lungs" provide the conditions for life on this planet. Unable to understand that human beings are interconnected with plants and animals by a holistic intelligent system, civilization finds no reason to hear the alarm, rise to the occasion and change its direction.

Society always wants to believe everything is normal right to the end. There is always plenty of time to manage the big crises. History has repeatedly shown this same pattern. Today's governments assume – or hope – that technology and big Ag with its ever more lethal pesticides and genetically modified organisms will find a way to manage crises like climate change and food insecurity. Like Ponzi schemes that eventually come crashing down because the resources to shore up non-existent accounts finally dry up, we are fast coming to the end of the robbing Peter to pay Paul pattern of our global economy. Humanity has come to the crossroads. We can choose to wait until events descend on us or we can create a new way of living based on collaboration, respect and whole system solutions.

While most people seem largely unaware of the coming storm, there is a segment of humanity that doesn't need convincing. With sea levels rising and droughts doubling down, many of us can sense the ominous events heading our way. With an abundance of clear and undeniable facts, Rennie speaks plainly and calmly about the current time (a time like no other) we live in. With society believing that everything is fine and preferring to change nothing fundamentally, he calls on the New Humanity to turn on its ignition switch and come together. Now is the time to create brilliant new-living options that deliver a new promise for the future of humanity.

Even if society stays tightly bound to its unsustainable course right to the end, The New Humanity movement can still create a pathway out of the impasse that others can follow. Coming events will turn public attention our way when we can dramatically showcase how to live and thrive ourselves. Presenting a roadmap for changing the future, Rennie inspires new thinking for creating new solutions for a momentous opportunity that can transform the whole paradigm.

This first book takes us back to the amazing time when change swept the North American continent. A gift to those who yearn to change today's world, it returns to Our Roots, not to make a new record about a largely forgotten history, but to inspire a new generation to realize how social change happens when a movement chooses to step out from under the radar and unite to change the world.

Rather than feel discouraged by the fear and division sweeping the land, we need to realize how many we are. There are tens of millions of us. We are the ones we have been waiting for. I see it everywhere I go.

The metaphor I use to describe our movement is that of a mycelial web. What is believed to be the largest organism in the world is located in the Pacific Northwest and spans 2.4 miles. A massive mycelial mat, it is comprised of a filament network capable of transporting information and nutrient across vast distances. While it is underground and thus invisible to all but a few who seek to discover its mystery, when conditions are right, the mycelium comes alive and out pop mushrooms. You can see expressions of our vast global network—the mushrooms of the New Humanity—everywhere: in the Women's movement, Indivisible movement, Permaculture movement, Transition Towns, Black Lives Matter, Water Protectors, Trump resistance movement, the conscious business movement, ecovillages, ecocities, alternative energy communities - many of them wonderfully documented by observant people like Paul Hawken in his book *Blessed Unrest*. We are all here and profoundly connected by our longing for a human society that is life-giving. Our common vision is that humanity can meet its needs and thrive without destroying the ability of future generations—and other species sharing this Earth with us. Realizing our common purpose and "popping out" to become the visible and powerful global family we are, we get to discover who we are—an unstoppable force that can rise to the occasion and change the world.

A movement to change the world is the story of our time. We are not the first movement in history. It has happened before. It happened with the Renaissance. It happened with the American Revolution. It happened with the Sixties. And it is happening again today. This trilogy is a roadmap for how we can do it—a GPS for how the spirit of humanity can rise to the occasion in the time that is coming. Events are coming that will ignite The New

Humanity to launch full throttle. We may not stop the coming storm but we can certainly change its outcome.

The New Humanity sets forth the proposition that changing the world can truly happen. If you feel touched by the inspiration and want to take its timely message to heart, Rennie and I look forward to joining you to seize the time, change the outcome and empower the dream of The New Humanity—whose timing is perfect!

—Kirsten Liegmann

INTRODUCTION

On the day this book was printed, Donald J. Trump was President of the United States and his White House had just delivered an unnerving shock to the world. The fear and divide suddenly enveloping the country felt like a new normal had set in following a great seismic shift. Watching the news, you could see for yourself. One segment of America seemed gleefully empowered while another felt the urgent imperative to push back hard. Those who perceived the greatest threat to the American union since the civil war were dumbfounded by those who celebrated the head spinning election of Donald J. Trump. While America energetically was no longer a country anymore, the largest movement to change the world in history had just ignited as well.

Movements have happened before but they are a rare social phenomenon. Looking back on their remarkable history, the Renaissance transformed the feudal order. The American Revolution defeated a colonial empire. The Sixties stood up to an entrenched racist culture while standing down a brutal war in Vietnam. While every student learns this history in high school, not everyone has realized that today's movement is larger than the Renaissance, the American Revolution and the Sixties combined.

When a movement first appears, it can seem to come out of nowhere. Before it ignites, everyone is at the starting gate but under the radar and unaware of what they are about to do. A public event typically turns the ignition switch that starts the engine and delivers the shock and awe of millions of people in resistance. Like an avalanche tumbling down a mountain with a force that takes out unmovable objects, pundits and authorities rarely see it coming.

Before the Renaissance ignited, few people thought they would transform a feudal order. When everyone in the thirteen American colonies was sitting on the fence undecided about opposing British rule, one man—his name was Thomas Paine—ignited the American Revolution with his incendiary pamphlet, *Common Sense.* In January 1960, no pundit predicted millions of people, most of them in the 20s, would change our history—until four black college freshmen quietly took their seats at an all-white lunch counter on February 1 to ignite one of our most powerful modern movements.

Donald J. Trump is today's ignition switch. The shock of a hard right turn at the top of the federal government has ignited women, Millennials, Generation Z, Boomers, blacks, Latinos, gays, liberals, progressives, free spirits, observant farmers, environmentalists, civil servants, scientists, professionals, international protestors, and many who never previously demonstrated but are in the streets today because they cherish their diversity, free speech tradition and Constitution that enshrined "We The People" to mean equality for all the people.

When movements ignite, nothing unites them faster than the arrogant authority who brazenly advances his repressive agenda. Undercutting the free press by asserting the media is "the enemy of the American people" and proclaiming the Trump anti-press campaign is "going to get worse every day" the White House has guaranteed that civil service professionals, celebrities, scholars and millions of citizens who extol the American founders for their checks and balances of any president claiming all power in a democracy will join our resistance.

With a monumental movement rolling down the mountain today, everything the Donald does now to upend the American dream strengthens our avalanche.

Many Democrats blame themselves for this sudden turn of events. When I review the many causes for this remarkable seismic shift, I see the top reason is easily traced to the transformation of the Republican Party. I have friends who belong to the Republican Party and voted for Trump. They would dismiss my perspective that the Republican Party is a wrecking ball to the fabric of society. While Republicans will be harshly condemned by future generations for eroding the American dream, no argument seems to sway the Republican mind today. Events are coming that will make the case for me that humanity is in trouble. When the consequences of how we live on Earth arrive to upend today's Republican mind-set that climate change is a hoax and conspiracy, I will still be a friend. I will still collaborate and work with my Republican associates when they are ready to drop the blame and join a community that can live sustainably.

History will show that deception was the leading strategy for Republican success over the past decade. A national political party that previously advocated for smaller government, lower taxes, individual liberty and the value of family ties was shoved by a hard right collective employing talk radio shows and a Fox news television network to advance a philosophy of fear and divide. Based partially on made up talking points, Republicans repeated their talking points about 'death panels' in Obamacare and 'voter fraud' sweeping the United States over and over. Fueling the anger of their white Republican base whose good paying jobs were fading away, voters turned out and Republicans took power. While passing laws that restricted democracy and penalized seniors and minority voters, the Republican Party constantly and shamefully demonized the president of the United States as well. Meeting as a national caucus on Barack Obama's inauguration day, the Republican Party pledged its allegiance to oppose every initiative coming from the country's first black President.

The Trump election was the culmination of this deep river of partisan divide plowing through a long tradition of compromise like a chasm separates a terrain into two separate realities.

I grew up in Virginia and lived on a farm. My neighbors would have loved a brash talking salesman like Donald Trump. I spent years in Ohio and Michigan as well where Trump voters got their first stimulating rush for their new political "champion." I know these voters and it is hard for me to give up on them. I also know they have been shamefully "trumped."

Abraham Lincoln once said you can fool some of the people some of the time but not all of the people all of the time. When this book first went to press, it seemed hard to imagine that the millions of voters who fell for this hoax, hook, line and sinker, would ever figure it out—that a hard right agenda to upend the American dream can never advance our forgotten Americans but could end the American promise for everyone.

The Republican Party wants America to believe they are merely engaged in normal partisan politics and that Donald Trump is only fulfilling his election promise to make America great again. Nothing in our history compares to the deception of dismantling the New Deal, lowering the protections of the EPA, ignoring the science of climate change and rolling back the clock to a time when white male elites ruled the United States by calling the agenda "make America great again."

Watching Fox News explain the massive resistance to this deception makes me smile.

As Fox commentators wonder out loud why millions of Americas are so upset, hundreds of thousands of protestors march and demonstrate. Fox News wants to believe this is the shenanigans of the Democratic Party busing and paying protestors to turn out spontaneously in hundreds of cities because Democrats cannot accept the results of a 'normal' election. Of course there is nothing normal about one political party coming to power to dismantle the American dream and eroding the truths we hold to be self-evident.

Many thoughtful observers evaluating the resumes of Trump's cabinet appointments or considering the implications of his executive orders know in their hearts the Trump deception must never be normalized.

With political side-taking moving dangerously towards two separate nations, the Trump nation celebrates and exaggerates its narrow victory while the majority nation feels rudely awakened by the hard loud thud on the floor of its cherished Republic.

Can uniting the country ever happen again? Is it possible that Virginia, Ohio, Michigan and Pennsylvania voters fooled by the hoax will figure it out—that their billionaire hero is a wrecking ball to America's immigrant tradition, government fiscal health, public school funding, free school lunches, national health insurance, clean drinking water and equality for all? In the near term, it seems unlikely. No argument dampens the enthusiasm of the core Trump voter. It doesn't seem to matter that no one in the White House is draining the swamp. The Republican Party doesn't care that no government can make America great again with fear and divide as the governing strategy. Republicans show no remorse either that every democracy that previously admired American Presidents has shifted to scorn or fear for today's President. Instead of noticing the world chorus of protest forming a massive Trump opposition, Republicans stay giddy about their control of the legislative and executive branches and hell-bent determined to erode America's integrity abroad while dismantling EPA protections at home. After all, Republicans are just fulfilling their election promise.

When facts and logic have no traction in the Trump nation, how can the voters ever figure it out?

President Trump has unleashed the coal industry to pollute the rivers and creeks of West Virginia while giving the green light to the petroleum industry to poison the drinking water of Missouri River's with crude oil pipelines known to leak. We will witness together what happens when voter's drinking water is poisoned by a Republican hoax. The sad news is harsh events upending people's lives may be required for the Republican world view to be Red State rejected.

For today's movement wanting to end the nightmare and change the Trump effect, I have written this trilogy. I believe we will be wise to open the treasure chest containing the vast Sixties know—how about an earlier movement stood down two centuries of segregation. When the Sixties movement went into rural Mississippi in 1964 to stand up to the KKK and local judges and policemen who assumed lynching black men and women could be done without consequences, we confronted their racism. Standing our ground, we were arrested and jailed. Some lost their lives. Singing, persevering civil rights activists stood down the extreme bigotry of a rural white culture and changed the United States.

Today's movement can learn from the Sixties as we prepare to change the world again.

Rather than join a pity party about today's hard right rise to power, it is time to realize what the Sixties movement discovered decades ago. When we left our conventional society to become a movement to change the world, we stopped being a tiny voice for hope and change. We were a movement now. We realized a movement is an avalanche that takes out walls.

During the 1960s, it took time for us to assume our full measure of influence and power. A thousand people marching in Birmingham in the early Sixties grew to 500,000 people marching in Washington, D.C. by the end of the decade. We had massive peaceful mobilizations like today but we had sit-ins and civil disobedience too. Both strategies were important and necessary. By 1970, college students closed down 90% of American universities with a national strike that spread to the military. Active duty GIs opposed the war policies of President Nixon too. By 1971, our movement shook the White House to its core with the largest civil disobedience arrest in American history. It took time for us to appreciate the value of organizations working in coalition—but we did. Today's movement can discover the power of coalition as well-by mobilizing two collaborating strategic waves: (1) millions of people who peacefully assemble and (2) massive nonviolent civil disobedience that closes the capitol building while the whole world is watching.

The banner that initially unites us today is to defend the best parts of the American dream and take back our country. To successfully initiative a second American revolution that restores the principle of We The People, we cannot be naïve about what that means either. It means organizing coalitions and activating tens of thousands of organizers who can turn our nonviolent resistance into lasting political change.

While the Democratic Party benefits from millions of people standing up for humanity, there is a culture that limits the Democratic Party. Fox News may want to believe the Democratic Party leads today's movement but it doesn't. A party of political liberals can become more progressive but it will not lead a movement to change the world. The Democratic Party may be part of the change but it is ill-prepared to mobilize women's marches around the world and civil disobedience in sanctuary cities. The Democratic Party will not end the careers of every elected Republican complicit in America's darkest hour by itself. We need an avalanche for that.

To appreciate the depths of our avalanche thundering down the mountain, realize there are three natural levels or components. The first level I call the *Resist and Reform movement*. Responding to the ominous national threat from Donald J. Trump, this component has been largely self-organizing with daily support from the media. As local communities turn out for Republican town halls with a relentless congressional advocacy, this component will evolve to include the resistance of civil service employees and White House boycotts of official dinners and ceremonies. This component understands Americans cannot be silent. This component realizes millions of voices defending the American dream can inspire thousands of women candidates to run for local, state and national office. This component will passionately oppose the deportation of 11 million immigrants, health care repeal, building the wall, deregulating the banks, drilling in wildlife preserves and dismantling the EPA.

A second wave—the *political revolution movement*—is also coming. The second wave will not erode the peaceful protests of the reform movement if it stays nonviolent. These activists will deepen the courage of the first wave with new forms of civil disobedience in sanctuary cities and traditional forms of civil disobedience in the D.C. offices of complicit Republicans. Following the footsteps of Martin Luther King, Jr and Mahatma Gandhi, this second component will mobilize depositors to withdraw from banks that fund the pipelines. This wave can mobilize 300,000 people to sit in Congressional offices while tens of thousands more sit in the streets and bridges carrying traffic to and from the White House. As a world television audience witnesses the U.S. government converting football stadiums into temporary prisons like they did for America's largest civil disobedience in 1971, these activists will bring hope to the world while experiencing the heart-warming support of Washington church leaders, D.C. universities and people who live in the nation's capital.

These two extraordinary components will be additionally supported by a third component I call *The New Humanity*. As one part of our movement resists the Trump assault on the fabric of the nation, another part will set up and get ready for the second challenge coming our way.

The consequences of how we live on Earth are coming for the present time.

I know it may seem hard to imagine that "climate change" will knock on our own door with a change that is sweeping and not modest. I realize society has yet to notice our oceans are dying. The New Humanity, however, understands we cannot survive as a species if we continue to ignore the human effect on our oceans, rain forests, diversity and eco-systems. Once "climate change" knocks, knocks, knocks, our movement will change, change, change. The moment will come when today's movement will look back on the Trump election and quietly feel a tinge of gratitude that he ignited our movement. The fact that we massively exist will seem like a blessing once we are forced to respond to our second challenge.

Today's movement was ignited by Donald J. Trump but tomorrow's movement will pioneer a new way of living on Earth.

The New Humanity is the one component of our movement that can see the distant horizon and realize a storm is coming—and that it is time to get ready now. The New Humanity has discovered how to live and thrive aligned with nature. The New Humanity knows how to create a new-living response that can support any region struggling to cope to live and thrive without destroying the planet. The new humanity may be the only ones who can.

When I say "climate change," I don't mean the single ominous challenge of rising sea levels threatening the world's coastal regions. I mean entire hemispheres massively disrupted by overpopulated inland urban centers like Mexico City running out of water and sinking. The New Humanity is the one segment of humanity that can look beyond the mockery of climate change deniers to notice and observe the rapid rate of melting glaciers at the Arctic and Antarctic ice cover happening today. The New Humanity understands the implications of the leading government declaring global warming is a conspiracy created by the Chinese and selecting the chairman of Exxon Mobil for its secretary of state.

In other words, The New Humanity can sense and feel the deep river beneath our current time. The New Humanity realizes the "Age of Man" has grown addicted to growth and consumption with little to no understanding that our civilization is unsustainable and passed the point of no return on climate change some time ago.

Damming up half the large rivers of the planet while cluttering and poisoning the rest of our world with plastics, metals, chemicals, housing sprawl, unsustainable agriculture and an indifference to the intelligence of nature, the consequences of how we live on Earth has a trajectory that sadly targets our own present time.

Harsh events are gathering for today's generation. Society will ignore the scientists sounding the alarm until climate change knocks, knocks, knocks. Before it's too late, The New Humanity has the foresight to get ready now.

With the sixth great extinction of species fully under way, the planet's stable climate patterns and resource abundance that once favored the age of man are rapidly fading into oblivion. Society may want to believe everything is normal but a segment of humanity knows better. The New Humanity is already assembling a new-living nation for a journey to evolve. While civilization continues to promote its endless growth and consumption model, Arnold Toynbee's history of collapsed civilizations has issued a warning. A civilization in trouble always believes everything is fine right to the end.

The New Humanity has reviewed the science to reach its own conclusion. Civilization is unsustainable. Humanity has come to the crossroads. What we do or fail to do in the next few decades determines our outcome.

Fortunately, the New Humanity has the know-how to restore the 24 million acres of topsoil annually blowing away and turn large bodies of polluted water into safe drinking water. The New Humanity component will be especially cherished by Trump voters who face the harsh reality of food insecurity. What inspires me most about The New Humanity is its ability not to be pulled in by the fear and divide. Solving problems without a need for finger pointing, The New Humanity replaces fear and divide with passion and collaboration. This third component is a welcomed addition to the largest movement in history.

We will have our different approaches to changing the world but respecting our differences and not turning on each other, we are a movement that can change the world. A future time will remember the present time as humanity's greatest generation. A future generation will remember that we were the generation that made America great again.

To end the nightmare of the Trump effect, we must realize it is not just the brain of Donald J Trump that seems devoid of respect, compassion, morality and kindness. There is a large segment of humanity trapped by their insecurities, negative egos, self-importance, victim worries, and the delusion that fear and divide can somehow better their own lives. Healing the separation and regenerating our humanity is the task of a new humanity when our family is hurting and struggling with fear.

Like Donald J. Trump, many voters are trapped in their head as well. While Trump's brain may be unreachable, it would be a mistake to assume every Trump follower is unreachable too. Many were simply upset by the indifference of the Democratic Party and voted for change. As Trump voters lose their cherished benefits and realize the consequences of Trump's affinity for Putin, movement bridge builders can connect with those who want a way out. If the voters feel support rather than name calling—or a moral superiority that casts them as idiots—valuable bridges can be built to the Trump nation itself.

In the course of my own life, I've made mistakes. Have you? Isn't our mission is to connect with anyone who feels ready to restore our humanity.

We need to realize that impeachment will not end the Trump nightmare. The Republican Party will wants to continue the nightmare. The vice president will become the new president. The hard right cabinet will remain in place. The Republican deception machine will continue to spin. When Trump is impeached, the energy of the movement may be temporarily deflated as well. While today's movement will survive one hapless White House replaced by another, the sooner we realize we are not going back to normal anytime soon, the stronger we become.

A movement to take back America will not end with impeachment.

Because today's movement stands on the shoulders of previous movements that set out to change the world, we should learn how they did it too. Have you ever wondered how the Sixties movement overcame the fear and divide of millions of racists who would die for their cause? Do you know how the Sixties movement would have dismantled the rise of anti-Jewish bigotry today?

It is time to discover the Sixties because it is so relevant again today.

History has shown that a united movement is an avalanche to feudal orders, imperial empires, and the arrogant captain of a ship of state. It is time for our movement to stand up for humanity. This trilogy explores our options including building a nation that shall not perish from the Earth. This first book returns to the Sixties to learn how we did it before so we can do it again today.

I grew up integrated into a mainstream society—until I said goodbye to conventional society and set out to change the world. It was 1960 and tens of thousands of young people were joining our movement. By the end of the decade, we had created a political and cultural revolution that upended many of America's most repressive traditions. The Civil Rights Act and Voting Rights Act became the law of the land and the Vietnam War ended as a result of massive pressure we and the Vietnamese brought to bear.

That's why I want to return to some of the most riveting stories of that decade—to glean insight and wisdom from these earlier experiences that might help us meet the unprecedented challenges we face today. This book is the story of how we did it then and how we can do it again today.

My own Sixties story began on February 1, 1960—the day four black teenagers decided to risk everything to change America.

I was a nineteen-year-old political science major at Oberlin College in Ohio. I had grown up on a farm in the Blue Ridge Mountains and got A's in high school, played on the basketball team, and was president of the student body. But my passion was a youth organization called 4-H. I prided myself on winning the Virginia State and East Coast contest for judging the production and health of chickens. In other words, I was a certified, full-fledged citizen of rural America. I thought of myself as a normal student in every way and certainly an unlikely candidate to be publicly singled out by Vice President Spiro Agnew, just a few years later, as "the most dangerous man in America." Anyone who knew me in high school would have laughed at the idea. But on that otherwise unremarkable Monday in February, my "normal" world was about to be turned upside down. Four courageous men in Greensboro ignited a brushfire in my mind that still burns today.

Having made their decision the previous evening to do more than just talk about achieving racial equality in America, Joseph McNeil, Franklin McCain, Ezell Blair, Jr., and David Richmond—all black college freshmen at North Carolina Agricultural and Technical State University—spent a fitful night filled with premonitions of beatings and arrest, or worse. In 1960, a host of repressive

"Jim Crow" laws were still on the books in North Carolina—and across the South—making it dangerous for any black person to attract the authorities' attention. A century after the Civil War, any black man or woman could still be lynched by a white mob in America. After class that afternoon, the four men met up in downtown Greensboro, walked anxiously together along South Elm Street, and then filed through the door of the landmark Woolworth's 5 and 10 store. There was nothing unusual in that. Black people were allowed to shop at Woolworth's for general merchandise. They could patronize a stand-up snack bar and order food. But the store's sit-down lunch counter was reserved for white customers only. Blacks could buy toothpaste alongside white people, but not order a hamburger and eat it where they might brush elbows with whites. The restaurant staff was also segregated: white people worked behind the counter while blacks did the cooking and cleaning out of sight in the kitchen. The infamous signs identifying which areas in the store were "whites only" or "colored only" had been taken down in 1958, under pressure from community civil rights activists, but that hardly mattered. Everyone knew the rule and no one dared challenge it, that is, until this day. The Greensboro Four, as they would later be called, gathered their courage, approached the lunch counter together and sat down. Expecting an immediate hostile reaction and surprised to be ignored by the waitress, they wondered why they were shunned. Perhaps people thought they were visitors from out of town and simply ignorant of local customs. The four dispelled any doubt about their purpose when they pointedly got the attention of the waitress, ordered food and drinks, and then refused to leave until they were served. The higher-ups decided to close the store early that evening, most likely in the belief that the "black troublemakers" would go home and have second thoughts, or get some sense talked into them by cooler heads. But they returned the next day. And the next. And the next—every day in fact for weeks, despite intense anger and even violence directed at them. Other protesters joined them at the counter, and a picket line formed outside the store. This simple, defiant act of taking a seat in a diner and ordering food quickly inspired others to hold similar "sit-ins" across the South. As the sit-ins grew in size, the Woolworth's company eventually grew tired of all the national negative attention. On July 25th, Woolworth's Department Store agreed to fully desegregate all its stores.

During those early months in 1960, when our resolute, non-violent protest was mobilizing, I was a college student watching the nascent Civil Rights Movement in America take a huge leap forward. I knew I was going to be part of it. I had gone to a segregated high school myself and remembered standing up in a social studies class to ask the teacher about the black high school on the other side of town. I also remember the chilly silence that fell over the classroom as I stepped into this forbidden taboo subject. Watching media coverage of events in Greensboro just a few years later, I was spellbound by what four students were able to accomplish by acting together and not giving in to fear, heckling, threats, and intense resistance, some of it from the black community itself. What might we achieve, I wondered, if our numbers were four thousand? Four hundred thousand? A million? Could we overcome racism in America altogether and stand down the entrenched legal system that had kept it in place? Something in me knew the answer. I was able to imagine an entire generation waking up out of a deep sleep. In early 1960, I could, before there was any evidence, sense that a vast population of college students was about to transform from an amorphous mass, uncounted and unheard, into a potent and powerful awakening giant—one that would arise and stir with a hunger for real change.

Nor did that unexpected prophetic vision remain "imaginary" for long. Over the next dozen years, people in their twenties came together in unprecedented numbers, inspiring millions of older adults to join in as well. Together, we formed the largest coalition for social change our nation had seen. We stood down legalized racial discrimination. We challenged income inequality, women's inequality, and a brutal war in Vietnam. I felt privileged to step out of a conventional society to be part of that tumultuous history. I felt honored to play a role in events that rewrote the American story. Overnight, I forgot all about my "4-H normal" world to become part of a national student movement for real change and justice. During the next decade, my focus and experiences included:

- Helping to organize the most significant student organization of our generation—Students for a Democratic Society (SDS)—with Tom Hayden and others
- Moving into a poor white Chicago neighborhood as an SDS community organizer where I was arrested the first night, sleeping in an apartment shared by other activists
- Mobilizing a thousand poor white people from Kentucky, Alabama, and Tennessee to join Dr. Martin Luther King,

Jr.'s open housing marches in an all-white Chicago neighborhood

- Watching some of my best friends beaten in the South for standing up to racism
- Visiting North Vietnam to see for myself the effects of U.S. bombing on civilian populations, to my government's disapproval
- Speaking to 150,000 people about my Vietnam experiences at our first antiwar mobilization on the Pentagon
- Coordinating the historic demonstrations during the 1968 Democratic National Convention in Chicago that dramatically shifted American public opinion about the Vietnam war
- Getting knocked unconscious by police in Chicago
- Being indicted and convicted as one of the Chicago Seven in a trial described by the *New York Times* as "the most significant political trial in U.S. history." My conviction was reversed on appeal.
- Receiving an invitation from the North Vietnamese government to return to Hanoi to bring U.S. prisoners of war back to their families
- Employing humor and fun during testimony at the House Un-American Activities Committee to shine a light on that Congressional committee's shameful witch hunt practices
- Living under twenty-four-hour surveillance by plain-clothed policemen, some of whom became good friends
- Helping organize the largest student strike in American history, encompassing 90 percent of the nation's college campuses
- Organizing a 1971 demonstration in Washington, D.C. that resulted in the largest civil disobedience arrest in American history, turning a D.C. football stadium into a temporary prison
- Partnering with John Lennon to tour the country staging rallies and concerts against the Vietnam War
- Experiencing firsthand the passion, love, and courage of an entire generation committed and determined to change the world

Without a doubt, the Sixties was a unique juncture in American history—fascinating and fruitful years of tremendous social growth. Like other great social movements in history—the Renaissance and the American Revolution, for instance—the energy and momentum of the Sixties seemed to bubble up unexpectedly out of the ground to sweep us along in its current. In roughly a decade, the United States was yanked from an entrenched cultural oppression of Afro-Americans into a greater awareness of injustice, inequality, and individual liberty. I witnessed firsthand the power of ordinary people to reshape a public agenda. I became part of a grassroots revolution that forever changed the way we think and act as a nation. I also became one of the recognizable "faces" of the Sixties movement. People saw me on the news speaking at rallies attended by thousands, on trial following the historic protests in the Democratic Convention in Chicago, and at the center of a global media storm when I returned from Hanoi with P.O.W.s whom the North Vietnamese Government would release only to me.

If anyone today might be tempted to cling to the importance of the Sixties and rest on the laurels of all that we accomplished, it might be me—but that is not why I wrote this book.

I have no need to look backwards or return to the past. In the pages ahead, I will share my Sixties story in order to pass on some of the important, forgotten lessons of how we did it.

This book is for a new generation poised to take up the task of changing the world again. My purpose is not to tell the "real" story of the Sixties, or take the reader behind the scenes, or defend what we did as if mistakes were never made. My interest is the present time and to explain how the puzzle of the Sixties actually came together: why millions of young people left society to change the world and how we can and must do it again.

Vietnam was an important part of that story too. A developing peasant country was able to stand down the world's most advanced military power. How that happened has relevance today as well. In a time of fear and divide enveloping the planet, could hundreds of millions of people collaborate again for the sake of humanity today? Understanding that the transforming event of our world is not behind us but right in front of us, a return to the story of what happened decades ago in the United

States and Indochina may help us realize that it is truly possible to change the world today.

Simply put, I have written this book more than fifty years after the Greensboro Four signaled the start of a powerful mass movement to change the world—because we must do it again.

When future historians look back on the present time to understand how our thoughts and actions shaped our current crisis, they will not linger long on the Sixties. The events of the twentieth century—two world wars, the Great Depression, nuclear proliferation, and the collapse of the Soviet Union—will seem irrelevant to them. The only relevant issue any future generation will remember will be what we did or failed to do in the present time. This is our time. This is humanity's time. This is the time for a global movement to write a new human story.

Society's solutions for today's mounting environmental problems are unfortunately too little, too late. Governments may set new environmental standards to lower carbon emissions but no government can stop the storm that is coming—the immigration from broken nations, the death of the oceans and the vast ecosystem collapse redefining the future of our world. Multinational corporations will seek technology solutions but like the Democratic Party they will not lead humanity to a new way of living either. Trapped by their unsustainable commerce, they will mostly protect their investments and established practices.

It is easy to fear that the forces of darkness will win the day but our time is pregnant with a human transformation far exceeding anything we dreamed of in the Sixties. In fact, the people who created the Sixties movement are mostly still here. Many have quietly continued to work for a better world, and will join in again. But it is up to a new generation—as it was in the Sixties—to provide the passion and creativity that ignites the change so urgently needed now. Some pundits will say Millennials are too indifferent to change the world but millions of people in their twenties know something is deeply flawed and that it is their time to reverse course on an unsustainable civilization and change the outcome of humanity.

This trilogy of books is a manual for how that can happen. This trilogy goes back to the Sixties for valuable lessons pertinent to the present time and looks to a future when a global movement builds a nation that changes the world.

In 1971, John Lennon told me he was ready to lend his voice to the American antiwar movement. The Beatles had disbanded and John was heading in new directions with his music and his life. John and I worked together, planning a forty-two-city tour in the U.S. in which his music and our message would unite. We wanted to reignite the student fervor that was beginning to wane. Our initiative ended abruptly after one rally in Michigan when the U.S. government began deportation proceedings against John.

That is how I came to be sitting in John and Yoko's Manhattan apartment one afternoon in July when he looked at his watch and realized he was late for an appointment. We jumped into his rented limo, and a short ride later, walked through the side door of The Record Plant, a state of the art recording studio just a few blocks from Times Square. Yoko Ono was already there, along with legendary record producer Phil Spector and members of the Plastic Ono Band, musicians who performed with John after the breakup of the Beatles. Without fanfare, John sat down at the grand piano and began recording the final overdubs of a new song scheduled for release that autumn. It had a haunting, simple melody, and his voice seemed to me more earnest and vulnerable than ever before.

The lyrics especially moved me. After all my years in a movement for change, the message of this song embodied—and somehow, transcended—what I had worked for through all the rallies, trials, sit-ins, freedom rides, arrests, and beatings; all the press conferences, Vietnam trips, mobilizations, and successes and failures. John managed to sum it up in three minutes of musical magic with one song called "Imagine".

Imagine there's no heaven
It's easy if you try
No hell below us
Above us only sky
Imagine all the people living for today

Imagine there's no countries
It isn't hard to do
Nothing to kill or die for

And no religion, too
Imagine all the people living life in peace

You, you may say I'm a dreamer
But I'm not the only one
I hope someday you'll join us
And the world will be as one

Imagine no possessions
I wonder if you can
No need for greed or hunger
A brotherhood of man
Imagine all the people sharing all the world
You may say I'm a dreamer
But I'm not the only one
I hope someday you'll join us
And the world will be as one*

That's what this trilogy is about—a call to imagine a new human story. It is the last call for humanity, but it comes with a roadmap for seizing the moment and pioneering a dream. The New Humanity is tens of millions of people who believe all the people can share and cherish all the world. What's more, we are showing ourselves that we can rise to the occasion and change the outcome.

The New Humanity is the story of a movement to change the world. It is about the extraordinary global pioneers who set out on a journey to evolve and end up changing the entire human condition. It is the story of our time.

*Reprinted with permission from Downtown Music Publishing.

Chapter 1
MEMORIES

Farm Boy to Activist

I was born in Lansing, Michigan but can't remember my first two years at all. I barely recall my grade school years either. Except for a few nostalgic images and reminiscent memories, what mostly stands out for me about my childhood is not how much I remember but how little I can recall. Why it is that childhood memories are so easily lost has been a mystery for me. When I reach back to see my own past, I see a mostly blank slate. The first vivid impression I had was of my own family moving into rural Virginia after seventh grade. That's when my memories finally became keepers.

I moved to a place where nothing much changed either. Sleepy hollows and normal neighbors are where my own story begins.

Since this is a book about changing the world, why start where time is frozen and change rarely budges an inch? Because of the Sixties, I have learned to appreciate that normal sleepy places sometimes are the birthplace of revolutionaries who change the world like rural Virginia where I grew up as a teenager.

I lived on a farm surrounded by oak trees, gentle mountains and a close-knit family of two parents, John and Dorothy, my elder brother, Dick, two younger brothers, Bob and John, and my sister, Bea, all of us tightly bound and living together inside a log cabin. We joked and laughed and were competitive, but always found ways to get along. Tied at the hip until we graduated from high school, each of my siblings left the Blue Ridge Mountains, one by one, to join a movement that changed the world. Years later, even my parents joined the Sixties movement too.

Decades later, when my brother John purchased ten acres close to where we grew up and arranged a family reunion, he gave me a second chance to realize rural Virginia still held memories of my roots.

Coiner's Department Store

Clarke County Historical Association Photo

Rediscovering that Virginia was my home was not as melodramatic as that black minstrel song sung by homesick Confederate soldiers who longed for "old Virginny"—but it made me appreciate why people who once lived on remote farms can get drawn to a place out of time that rarely changes. You can get a clear picture of an unchanging world by visiting Main Street in Berryville, twelve miles from our Virginia farm. One of my memories about Berryville was sitting on a drugstore barstool after school with a chocolate, marshmallow, and peanut ice cream sundae called a "CMP." After the treat, I would cross the street and visit the town's department store to watch their employees' remarkable way of doing business. Sometime in another century, a pulley contraption attached to a long wire was installed and stretched through the merchandise room up to the second floor bookkeeping department. A customer writing a check would hand the payment to the clerk who would place it in a tiny container on a wire connected to the second floor. When the clerk pulled down on the wooden handle, the container fired like a rocket to the second floor where the transaction got recorded. Any change got counted out and put back in the cup and shot back to the salesperson like a pinball. The store owner managed this archaic business museum until he was in his nineties.

The whole town was like this department store. Everyone had their story and everyone knew everyone else's stories as well. Jane's Lunch opened in 1942 and never changed its mid-twentieth century American Southern diner décor at all. The food was often compared to a cafeteria and the staff was super nice, reinforcing the belief that people in the South are friendly. Many people who lived near Berryville in the countryside had large homes, some of them dating back to the Civil War. They were friendly too and their stories never changed much either.

In other words, I grew up with friendly, normal people but wound up joining a movement to change the world. During the 1960s, it seemed as if an entire generation had some version of this story. An entire generation packed up their normal lives and headed out to stand down an American racist culture. I remember watching our parents wring their hands as they watched us leave our normal lives to join a revolution.

Since coming events are about to repeat this Berryville story again, regular people will be riding the winds of change once more. That's one of the reasons I wanted to start my own Sixties story by starting with this important reminder: dreamers and visionaries, change-artists and revolutionaries, in every generation of history, have come from places where people had regular, everyday lives. It has happened before, and it will happen again today.

The place where I drove my first car—it was a sleek green Plymouth with a Hollywood muffler—was located between Berryville and the Appalachian Trail near the Shenandoah River. John Denver professed his love for this area in his song "Take Me Home, Country Roads". When he and I went to the Brazil Earth Summit together, I had to set the record straight. Since only a mere twenty miles of the Shenandoah flowed through West Virginia, I joked with John that it was Virginia—not West Virginia—that should have been given the credit in his famous song.

The county where I lived was named after General George Rogers Clarke who, like me, was one of those unlikely U.S. revolutionaries too. Clarke County had been carved out of a five-million-acre property owned by Lord Fairfax, whose home town was White Post. George Washington came to White Post to survey the area for Lord Fairfax where he met Daniel Morgan, who started out normal as well but eventually became another revolutionary hero from this rural area. Where I grew up, a small rural county had embedded a giant revolutionary history. When Daniel Morgan returned to the area after distinguishing himself in the American Revolution, he built a remote cabin in the woods that reminded people of that Daniel Boone story about the virtues of living far from every neighbor. According to our Virginia neighbors, the log cabin Morgan built was where my family lived when I was a teenager. With a broken down stone wall that once served people to grind their grains or vote in an election, our home—Morgan's Mill Farm—had its revolutionary story too.

General Morgan's Log Cabin

My Dad bought this 502-acre farm for a weekend retreat when he worked with President Truman's Council of Economic Advisers. When Dwight Eisenhower became president, however, he lost his position and moved to this remote Virginia location. How remote was it? I could buy a tank of gas or a loaf of white bread at Tinsman's tiny store a quarter-mile down the road from our cabin, but if I wanted to purchase something from a "real store," I had to cross the Shenandoah River and drive twelve miles to Berryville.

Formally established on January 15, 1798, Berryville had a robust twenty-five homes, three stores, a pharmacy, two taverns, and a school by 1810. It was not much bigger when it was named the county seat of Clarke County in 1836—or for that matter when I attended high school a century later.

Our farm was about a dozen stone throws from the Appalachian Trail and was not particularly crowded with hikers most of the year. But in the fall when canopies of trees displayed the vivid colors of the rainbow, many people hiked the fifty-four-mile trail that passed near our farm as they journeyed from Northern

Virginia to the Shenandoah National Park. When a person walked this enchanted trail, anywhere they looked, they could see animal tracks or the scat of bobcats. Sometimes, the smell of a striped skunk was present, and there were always deer, gray squirrels, groundhogs, and rabbits galore. As a teenager surrounded by nature and wild beauty, I confess I took this Virginia wonderland for granted. The oak trees, lespedeza grass fields, natural springs, and mountain streams running through the woods rarely put me in a state of breathless awe the way they did when I returned for the family reunion.

As a teenager, I grew up in a sleepy hollow surrounded by a ring of mountains where wild turkeys, deer, and some fifty different species of mammals made their homes. For me, it was just the way life was. With no comprehension of how special the Blue Ridge Mountains were, I was a 15-year-old sleepwalker largely unaware of the magical nature around me.

Normal places often harbor normal people who sleepwalk through their life until they wake up.

How sleepy was my teenage phase? I had no clue that European settlers had significantly diminished the natural species of the area. I never thought about the American bison that were eliminated in 1798 or the elk that disappeared in 1855.

Beaver and river otter were gone by the late 1800s and the eastern timber wolf, cougar, the white-tailed deer, turkey, black bear, and bobcats drastically declined as well. As a teenager, I knew nothing about this extraordinary species loss. With chores to do, I took this natural oasis around me for granted as I strolled through this beautiful rural countryside unaware and unconcerned.

I did realize my mountain neighbors were storybook characters—and I was seriously impressed with for their ability to spit tobacco over great distances. I got along with them too, even the skinny, shy Poocham, who rarely spoke a word when he lived on our farm and helped with the chores. On warm summer evenings, he would sit on his porch and play a haunting banjo tune whose tinny sounds cascaded through the hollow with bouncing echoes. If I tried to get closer to hear the music better, he would always disappear into his house.

Among my closest neighbors, the skilled woodsman, Herbert Tinsman, and the area's moonshine legend, Harvey Trussle, were my best friends. Harvey had fourteen children and made sure that once a month, one of them got to visit the "big" town of Berryville. Harvey had long legs so keeping up with him in a large hay field while turning the handle of a grass seeder was hard to do. Herbert, who preferred the name Tick, was a master with the axe and wise in the ways of nature. He lived in the unincorporated community of Frogtown which had one tiny store, a one-room church and a couple of houses. I did my best to understand what people in Frogtown were saying because they spoke with a sixteenth-century Elizabethan English accent using a Southern twang. They had their own way of talking. For example, when someone from Frogtown felt fear, he was described as "more scared than a long tail cat in a room full of rocking chairs."

Growing up, the two Potter brothers who cut my hair in Berryville were the only Afro-Americans I knew. The black community, with its racially segregated Johnson-Williams High School, was mostly invisible to the all-white segregated side of town. As a teenager, I thought of myself as awake and alert, but looking back, I would say I slept through the nightmare of this racist tradition.

I could make excuses. I could say I was just a teenager. But the fact is I lived in a rural county that had its dark secrets I never bothered to notice.

My dad purchased the Berryville Feed Store which was a county hub for local farmers. While I never chewed tobacco myself, many customers did, especially when spinning one of their hard-to-believe tales. When a railroad car unhooked at our store, twenty-thousand pounds of feed in 100 pound bags had to be unloaded and stacked to the ceiling. That was my job and it kept me in shape like no other time I can remember. Along with the feed store, Morgan's Mill Farm had chores too. It was not a hobby farm either. Large fields of grass to mow, hay to haul, sheep to shear and a chicken house with 6,000 tiny chicks under heat lamps growing to four-pound boilers in ten weeks meant morning and evening chores were piled on high school classes and homework.

Before the Sixties Movement, my idea of a student movement was 4-H clubs. Among the activities of this national youth organization, poultry judging was the one that appealed to me. I got to rank the egg production of hens and defend my decision before a panel of judges. Designed to teach the principles for grading the quality of living birds and applying USDA standards to ready-to-cook poultry and eggs, I learned a valuable know-how for judging chickens.

For example, a laying hen starts her egg production with a yellow skin pigment that bleaches out in an orderly process as she lays her eggs. The bleaching starts and stops as egg production begins and ends with each molting season. The skin pigment bleaches in a particular order too. Knowing the order, I could estimate the number of eggs a hen had laid since she molted. It was an awesome advantage when judging laying hens. When the yellow vent of the hen had completely bleached out, she had laid five to ten eggs. When her eye ring was bleached, ten to fourteen eggs had been laid, and so on until the back of the shanks and the hock joints were bleached at more or less 180 eggs.

The first time my picture was published in a newspaper, I was on the front page of the *Clarke County Courier* for earning the individual highest score for poultry judging in the county. Our team won first place too. For my first media debut, I was holding a chicken that the whole county—except myself—could see had just pooped on my pants. Like a teenage horror show, there I was grinning with my pooped-on pants on public display. I got over it only by winning the Virginia state contest and the U.S. East Coast contest. In Berryville, everyone seemed to forget that front-page embarrassment when chicken judging made me somewhat popular in the county.

During this time, I stuck to my chores like a born-again missionary and joined extracurricular school activities as well. Since I had hundreds of hours of practice time shooting hoops in our barn, I went out for varsity basketball and made the team. Then I became editor-in-chief of our high school paper, *The Breeze.* When I was elected school president, the student body in Clarke County High School met once a month in a large auditorium to make "student decisions". I thought the concept was inspiring but noticed it made my high school principal anxious. When I promoted a Saturday night program where teenage couples could dance outside the school's authority in a downtown Berryville hall, that stirred the hornets' nest. With virtually every student in high school supporting our "rebel" plan, my proposal to dance with no school authorities in sight received a resounding student affirmative vote.

In my first experience with student politics, I learned the importance of having large numbers in support when promoting a good cause.

Rural life was hard work with fun moments. On the Shenandoah River during the summer, Watermelon Park offered a break with live music, family barbeques, and river rafting. I went one weekend to hear someone named Johnny Cash who was dressed in solid black from head to toe—black shirt, black pants, black belt, black socks, black boots, and definitely looking good in black. That event is still talked about today. Watermelon Park was an outdoor festival that drew people from outside the area. During the summer the Park hosted celebrities like Patsy Cline, who lived in nearby Winchester and Dolly Parton, Flat and Scruggs, and the Stanley Brothers.

Where I was growing up, our small rural county was making some big music history.

Looking back on this "normal" sleepy time, I decided the universe must be a little rascal. Today I am listed as one of Berryville's notables. For a Chicago Seven defendant to become a notable in Berryville, Virginia should make any native chuckle. That was funny and definitely the handiwork of some little rascal.

The year I graduated from high school I had the opportunity to make a commencement address about the issues facing the future of our class. That was the year I was completely clueless that thirteen-year-old Betty Kilby had just become a plaintiff in a case designed to desegregate nearby Warren County public schools. Her case set off a firestorm of resistance. The Virginia governor wanted to close public schools rather than integrate them. I never got to meet these two amazing Virginia heroes, Betty Ann Kilby and her father—a proud farmer and grandson of a slave who believed education was central to his children's future. He was the driving force behind the case of Betty Ann Kilby vs. Warren County Board of Education that represented black children across the United States. Betty won her case too and had to push through a crowd of angry white classmates screaming racial slurs as the National Guard tried to restrain the crowd on her first day at an "integrated" school. Banned from sports and unable to go to the prom, she was harassed by her classmates while her teachers looked the other way. Shots were fired into her home and a cross burned on her lawn.

Cattle were mutilated as a warning. Betty Kilby was raped by white male students at her own school too.[2]

When I left Berryville for college life, only then did I begin to understand the sleepwalking nature of my "normal" teenage years. I never realized that enslaved blacks represented 55 percent of Clarke County's population before the Civil War. I never appreciated that former slaves were never "free and equal" after the war of "emancipation" either. National legislation like the Civil Rights Acts of 1866 and 1875 along with the Fourteenth and Fifteenth Amendments to the U.S. Constitution were passed, but state and federal court decisions stripped that "freedom" bare of meaning with their declaration that public facilities were "separate but equal". The laws that legalized Virginia's great racial divide drew their authority from the 1867 Dred Scott decision when the U.S. Supreme Court ruled that blacks were an "inferior and subordinate class of beings". Compared to other southern states, Virginia earned a reputation for having more harmonious race relations, but no one would understand why reading the twenty-five Jim Crow laws enacted in Virginia between 1870 and 1960. Jim Crow was only repealed by the 1964 Civil Rights Act, and even then, the entrenched racial prejudice of the white culture lived on.

Where I lived in rural Virginia, black people had to go to the back of the bus and stand up if there were not enough seats for whites to sit down. They had separate sections in libraries and train stations too. They were not allowed to use white water fountains or order food where whites ate. They were barred from beaches and swimming pools. Theater sections were reserved for whites only. Schools like Clarke County were not only segregated, local officials authorized less funding for black schools as well. As

2 Betty Kilby was a thirteen-year-old plaintiff who expressed in open court her desire for equal education. Her story is documented in *Wit, Will and Walls: The Betty Kilby Fisher Story*, a film based on her book. Her father was the driving force behind Betty Ann Kilby vs. Warren County Board of Education.

black education resources ran down from neglect, black teenage social life and black sports teams were punished as a way of life.[3]

I learned some of this history from Arthur K. Pope, who sent me an email the day I began writing this book. He wanted to interview me for his own book, *Carry Me Back,* that described his journey back to his Berryville family roots. He sent me a few draft chapters that opened my eyes.[4] Thomas Gold, in his *History of Clarke County,* had a similar impact. When the civil war "ended," Christian charity and neighborly love in the white community screeched to a stop at the gate of Berryville's black settlement. White people had little or no social interaction with the black community for the next century because that was "the custom".

I never abandoned my love for rural Virginia, but regret my ignorance of its troubling past when I lived there. White people in the area believed one part of Berryville was superior to another. That was "their custom." Betty Kilby who lived next door to me chose to change the custom and make a difference by standing up to this entrenched culture. I was unaware of her bravery as I went sleepwalking through my normal life.

Waking up is hard to do. That's one of the reasons these Sixties stories are so relevant today. The Sixties was a time when millions of people did wake up and set out to change a thousand normal places like Berryville, Virginia. We stood together in solid ranks and solemnly pressed for change. It seems hard to imagine that a place like rural Clarke County could harbor anyone who would join a movement to change the world but many did—and I was one of them. Just because a normal place believes nothing ever changes doesn't mean it never will. Changing normal places happens. And a very big change is coming again. This time the change that is coming will be sweeping and dramatic like no other time in history.

Today's troubled world is facing a steep climb. In every normal place and sleepy hollow, difficulties will be mounting. As we face the harsh consequences of how we live on the planet, no one should give up on a place like Berryville. When sweeping change

---

3 Kalbian, Maral S. *Clarke County: Images of America*. Charleston, SC: Arcadia, 2011.

4 Arthur K. Pope. Carry Me Back: A*n American Journey in Time and Place*. CreateSpace, 2015.

envelops sleepy towns, people wake up and revolutions spring forward. A movement to change the world can find revolutionaries in normal, sleepy hollows.

Chapter 2
THE SIXTIES

A Movement Takes Shape

Many people try to organize a movement but fifty years into their effort, they are still talking to each other about organizing that movement. Organizing a movement is no guarantee it will ever happen. Movements are a phenomena that seem to have a mystical quality. When a movement to change the world first appears, something unusual is afoot. Before a movement even starts, its vast constituency is at the starting gate—but under the radar and invisible to those who are about to change the world. That was our reality in January, 1960. One month before the Sixties revolution launched, we literally walked right by each other every day, unaware we were a movement that would change everything. No pundit predicted millions of people in their twenties would turn a racist culture upside down and challenge the entire political status quo of the nation. Only a handful of intuitive people sensed what was coming. Since I was one of them, that may be my only qualification for making this prediction now.

The largest movement in history is igniting today. It holds the promise of changing the outcome of the entire human condition.

In the late Sixties, I was privileged to be part of one of history's extraordinary movements. I was the coordinator of the largest coalition of antiwar and civil rights organizations during the most dramatic mobilizations of that era. I was co-director of the historic demonstrations at the Democratic National Convention in Chicago. I coordinated the largest civil disobedience arrest in American history and was a full-time activist who joined millions of others as we rolled down the mountain like an avalanche. When the Sixties movement ignited, we were civil rights activists, antiwar activists, college and high school activists, new culture hippies, Yippies[5], Latinos, farm workers, welfare mothers, poor white working people, antiwar Vietnam veterans, and peace and women's activists, united in our support of a new black leadership that would not back down. We were an overnight social phenomenon powered by three great waves that swept North America like a tsunami.

Our first wave gathered its force out of an intense social and political awakening about America's worst behavior—racism, economic inequality, voter suppression, arrogant Americans abroad, and a Cold War foreign policy that enflamed political witch hunts at home. Similar to today's women's march and campaign for Bernie Sanders, our first wave was energized by people who were waking up from the nightmare of southern lynchings and the shameless parade of Jim Crow laws. We quickly found the courage to stand down any authority that clung to second-class status for black Americans. By the mid-1960s, our focus on civil rights continued as we expanded our movement to end a war in Vietnam. When the U.S. military got bogged down in a Southeast Asian war that seemingly had no end even with nearly 500,000 U.S. soldiers in combat, the Vietnam War was seen by our movement as a misguided foreign policy, having no place in America's core values. Our "political wave" was successful too, mobilizing millions of people to stand down an entrenched racist culture and stop the Vietnam War. By the end of the decade, we had grown into tens of millions of activists—and most of us were in our twenties.

The second wave—the largest by far—emerged more playfully as young people abandoned their parents' career plan to pursue their own lives. Easily distinguished by how we dressed, looked, and acted—long hair, free-spirited, and open-curious—our youth culture ignited a generation gap that upset our parents and troubled society. People in their twenties were transformed coast to coast into free-spirited, free-love "hippies" and anywhere anyone looked, we were there, everywhere. A Woodstock Music and Art Fair held on a 600-acre dairy farm in the rural town of Bethel, New York, in 1969 brought 500,000 of us from every corner of the country to one rural location. Undeterred by the

---

5 Originally a term for the Youth International Party, it came to refer to any politically active hippie in the late '60s.

mud and rain, Woodstock became an unprecedented massive musical weekend that no one had fully envisioned. Woodstock symbolized the free-spirit nation of our entire generation.

Imagine if you can tens of millions of people in their twenties dropping out of society's collective assumptions to unlock their own passion. That's what the Sixties did. Our passion was blooming too. Passion didn't mean we had to be reckless or foolish either. Passion was about the way we felt inside. Millions of people uncorking their "Wild Thing" took a stroll through an American decade with an openness and confidence that proudly proclaimed, "I am not afraid to act and engage this world." There was no intellectual formula. It was all about our own self-image. The passion to do what we loved had nothing to do with being financially well-off either, or being the most intelligent or best educated. We simply followed our passion by pursuing something we loved, even when it wasn't all worked out in the beginning. We flipped a switch, got fired up, and set out to make our dreams come true. Many in the second wave of our movement experimented with pot and hallucinogenic substances, seeking to find magical experiences in inner realms. We played at the edge of an inner world where some even discovered the power of their own perception to influence and shape their outside world.

Empowering these two great waves—the "political movement" and the "hippie free love movement"—was another game changer called Rock 'n' Roll. The music of the Sixties broke down all social barriers like a mudslide takes out a concrete wall. In a time of cultural upheaval in attitudes, fashion, and beliefs, our Sixties music turned into a revolution itself. Some of the biggest performers came out to sing at our demonstrations, too. They marched with us and went to jail with us. Others created top-selling albums that ruled the airwaves while shaking up the complacency.

What's That Sound?

Janis Joplin
David Fenton Photo

Arlo Guthrie
David Fenton Photo

Jerry Garcia

David Fenton Photo

Mick Jagger

David Fenton Photo

From the iconic Bob Dylan to the worldwide Beatles phenomenon, the artists pioneering the Sixties revolution read like a Who's Who of rebels with a cause—Elvis Presley, the Rolling Stones, Fats Domino, Neil Young, Peter, Paul and Mary, Little Richard, Jimi Hendrix, Cream, the Supremes, Stevie Wonder, Aretha Franklin, Led Zeppelin, Ray Charles, Otis Redding, Sly and the Family Stone, Smokey Robinson, Sam Cook, the Doors, James Brown, Pink Floyd, Jefferson Airplane, Joan Baez, Judy Collins, Country Joe and the Fish, the Mamas and the Papas, Phil Ochs, Pete Seeger, Donovan, Herman's Hermits, Janis Joplin, the Grateful Dead, Big Brother and the Holding Company, Buffalo Springfield, Bob Marley and the Wailers , B.B. King, Rod Stewart, Howlin Wolf, the Byrds, the Beach Boys, Simon & Garfunkel, the Who, and Crosby, Stills & Nash—to name a few who transformed the Sixties into the most powerful music decade ever.

As a new generation rebelled and dropped out, we could hear the moans and pleas of our parents not to abandon the security of our promising careers. Because we had no steady jobs to support our "irresponsible and reckless lifestyle," our parents struggled to understand how we even survived.

One of the great secrets of the Sixties was how each of us had the other's back.

If I wanted to travel from D.C. to San Francisco, I simply walked out my front door and hitched a ride. I didn't need a bank account for coast-to-coast travel. I could stick out my thumb on any city street corner or highway for excellent results. Dressed in layers for all weather conditions—tie-dye T-shirt under a brightly-colored sweater covered with a working class coat—I preferred the green camouflage army jacket with toothbrush in pocket for long distance travel. It never took me long to catch a ride, either. Any van heading my way with painted flowers on the hood and music streaming out the window was guaranteed to stop. No one required a suit and tie to hitch a ride in America. The Beatles arrived from England in New York city. Everyone could plainly see who they were by how they looked.

A driver viewing me from his approaching car never had a doubt about my dream for a better world. When I left home to travel, I knew that in five minutes flat I would be riding in a vehicle full of passionate new friends. I eventually stopped being shocked when the destination of the hippie van that picked me up was the exact city I wanted to visit too.

Could a generational movement like the Sixties happen today? Today's movement will not be a retread of the Sixties but a second Sixties movement has started its engines. How will today's movement be different? For one thing, today's movement to change the world is larger. As we stop being invisible to each other, we will surprise ourselves with our sheer size, diversity, passion, and creativity. Once we fully ignite, we will feel staggered by the realization that we are the largest movement in history to change the world.

What causes a movement under the radar to ignite? Events sparked the Sixties just as events have sparked us today. While Trump voters love their champion for "understanding" their problems, it is Trump's Muslim bans and attacks on Latinos, women and gender equality that has become the ignition switch for today's movement. With his overreach of promises and disregard for the rights of all the people, our movement is underway. Trump's ignition is only the beginning too. Standing up for core human values will be followed by our global response to the harsh consequences of climate changes and the human effect destroying our planet.

Pure and simple, today's movement will face the consequences of how we live on this planet.

Harsh lessons are coming. Our initial movement launch will galvanize those who want to defend the American dream and take back their country. Many issues will start our avalanche down the mountain from the economic stratification into elites and "commoners" to the attacks on women, native American water rights, Muslims, blacks, Dreamers, and the LGBTQ community. But as the consequences of our unsustainable civilization arrive for all to see and experience, our movement begins a journey to evolve for a new way of living on Earth.

Like the Sixties, events will shape our destiny. The Sixties "snowball" down the mountain began with tens of thousands of students but grew into tens of millions of activists of every age. Once the Sixties movement became an avalanche, we did stand down entrenched segregation laws, hostile federal courts, congressional witch hunts, police brutality, and the considerable opposition of the Defense Department, White House, and U.S. Congress. Once we headed down the mountain, we grew by leaps and bounds too. When we met resistance from institutions invested in the status quo, our response was always the same. We never backed down.

Understanding how we did it is what makes the Sixties relevant again today.

Today's movement is similar to the Sixties movement in several ways. The Sixties movement had forerunners blazing the trail like today. Our forerunners today include Feel the Bern, Black Lives Matter, Standing Rock Water Protectors, the Permaculture movement, Occupy Movement, Democracy Spring, the environmental movement, LGBTQ movement and spiritual movement to name a few. Now that we've started, Trump will cause us to grow and expand. As we deeply realize we may be the last generation on Earth unless we change the world ourselves, our movement will eventually envelop the globe.

When the Sixties movement began, I was an undergraduate at Oberlin College waking up to the fact that white people in the South routinely murdered black people for wanting the same rights they expected for themselves. I joined with friends and formed a campus political party whose candidates for student government took stands for civil rights. We wrote letters and signed petitions to congressmen. We organized college-wide fundraising drives to support sit-ins in Tennessee. From Oberlin, Ohio, we bailed out arrested students in Mississippi by making pledges not to eat at certain times in the dining hall so we could send the saved money to civil rights sit-ins in the South. Watching the Greensboro sit-in movement spread through the South, it seemed natural to organize a new approach to student government. When we did, all our candidates won their first election too.

The Sixties movement began by turning a switch. When the Sixties switch went on, I was a sophomore at an institution that had been a leader in the U.S. abolition movement. During the Sixties, however, colleges that never took a stand championed the cause for civil rights. Students and faculty from hundreds of universities that never previously spoke out for social change joined our movement. People in the Sixties who never protested stepped forward for civil rights. People today who never spoke out are turning out to demonstrate in the millions. That's the mystical part.

When an undergraduate student from the University of Michigan visited me in Ohio my sophomore year, I learned from Tom Hayden that students in Ann Arbor had organized a campus political party as well. Tom suggested we should organize students coast to-coast and with that nudge of encouragement, we never looked back. Students for a Democratic Society (SDS) was launched and a student movement was born.

Tom Hayden was a gifted writer and drafted a manifesto called the *Port Huron Statement.* Robb Burlage and others helped finalize the document whose message inspired students to join the movement during the early Sixties. As students joined, our snowball down the mountain gathered momentum.

The *Port Huron Statement* was a 25,700 word pamphlet that inspired many to get off the fence. Presented to our first SDS national convention in Port Huron, Michigan, it called for participatory democracy "as a means and an end". It was an "Agenda for a Generation" in which racism and the Cold War were the two central issues. It argued that universally-controlled disarmament should replace deterrence as a national goal— and democratic institutions should empower publically-disinherited groups with voter registration drives and black political candidates. Metropolitan reform movements should take on undemocratic big city regimes with issues of peace and civil rights. Universities should be reformed with an alliance of students and faculty. Students and teachers should take back their university from government military research and administrative bureaucracies. The *Port Huron Statement* called on universities not to ignore major public issues but bring them directly into the curriculum without fear of debate.

In 1962, the *Port Huron Statement* was widely read on college campuses, putting to pen the salient reasons why a student movement was needed:

SDS Organizing Conference
Clark Kissinger Photo

- *"The American political system is not the democratic model of which its glorifiers speak. In actuality it frustrates democracy by confusing the individual citizen, paralyzing policy discussion, and consolidating the irresponsible power of military and business interests.*
- *"Our work is guided by the sense that we may be the last generation in the experiment with living."*[6]

After Oberlin College, Tom and I continued to work together. We traveled to North Vietnam together. We coordinated the historic events at Chicago's Democratic Convention together. We were co-defendants in the trial of the Chicago Eight. I agreed with the writer for *The Atlantic* who summarized Tom's impact on the nation with four words. "Tom Hayden changed America." Richard Goodwin had been a speechwriter for Presidents Lyndon Johnson and John Kennedy and believed Tom had "inspired the Great Society without even knowing it."

As SDS emerged as a new national voice for activist students on hundreds of northern colleges and universities, a second youth organization—the Student Non-Violent Coordinating Committee

6 The Port Huron Statement was adapted by a conference of Students for a Democratic Society in Port Huron, Michigan in 1962.

(SNCC)—was holding its first meeting at Shaw University in April, 1960. SDS felt an immediate alignment with SNCC. SDS wanted to support SNCC's full-time Southern activists who lived on $10 a week. SNCC organizers were mobilizing hundreds of students and non-students for sit-ins and freedom rides in Mississippi, Alabama, Georgia, Arkansas, and Maryland. SNCC also organized voter registration drives throughout the South, but especially in Georgia, Alabama, and Mississippi.

I watched local officials repeatedly confronted by SNCC's acts of courage. SNCC could turn the tide of a segregated business with its nonviolent sit-ins and boycotts of white-only retail facilities. Sit-ins were the initial main focus of SNCC and the early Civil Rights Movement until a small group of activists decided to embark on a "Freedom Ride" by boarding two buses from Washington, D.C. for New Orleans on May 4, 1961. It took commitment but thirteen people signed on as interracial passengers into a new American history.

The Supreme Court had declared that segregation in business terminals was illegal in *Boynton v. Virginia.* The Court outlawed racial segregation in restaurants and waiting rooms in interstate bus terminals and the Interstate Commerce Commission issued its own ruling against "separate but equal" interstate bus travel as well—but that hardly mattered. State Jim Crow laws controlled interstate travel in the South, and the federal government was powerless to enforce its own rulings. With government unable to enforce its own laws and rulings, the Sixties movement did what movements do—we acted where government could not—all by ourselves.

Whenever governments become gridlocked and self-serving, movements to change the world remove the roadblocks.

The first Freedom Ride was organized by James Farmer of the Congress of Racial Equality (CORE) with seven blacks and six whites. No government gave them permission to challenge the entrenched racist culture. One of the passengers was now—U.S. Congressman John Lewis. A student at Fisk University who had become a leader in the Nashville sit-ins and dedicated to the philosophy of nonviolence, he was jailed numerous times for de-segregating lunch counters in downtown Nashville. He inspired activists like me.

When the first group of Freedom Riders boarded the two interstate buses—Greyhound and Trailways—they headed straight into a southern taboo norm. Their itinerary took them from Washington, D.C. through Virginia, North Carolina, South Carolina, Georgia, Alabama, Mississippi, and Louisiana. Their plan was to end with a celebration rally in New Orleans.

The passengers scattered throughout the bus with one rider taking a seat in the far back to avoid arrest and arrange bail when everyone in the front was arrested. That was the movement's seating plan. Interracial pairs sat in adjoining seats, and one black rider took a seat in the first row reserved for whites. As the two buses headed out of Washington, D.C., Virginia and North Carolina, they met modest white resistance, but deeper into the South, white mobs were larger and violent. Despite federal laws to "protect" a citizen's right to travel, these passengers were beaten and arrested for unlawful assembly, trespassing, and violating state and local Jim Crow laws.

In Rock Hill, South Carolina where the Freedom Ride faced its first savage attack, John Lewis got off the bus and entered a white-only waiting room where he was viciously beaten by two men. Mob violence had been given a green light from local police officials. In Alabama, Bull Connor was an infamous Alabama police commissioner who joined a local police sergeant who was a vocal Ku Klux Klan supporter. Their plan was to inflict harsh violence against the Freedom Riders in Alabama before they were arrested to make certain Freedom Rides would permanently end. A hate mob was granted fifteen minutes by police to attack the demonstrators before the arrests. The pattern of mob violence that started in Anniston would finish the Freedom Ride off in Birmingham. That was the white supremacy plan.

On Mother's Day, the Anniston KKK—many still in their Sunday church suits—attacked the first Greyhound bus. The vehicle was forced to stop when an eighteen-year-old KKK ex-convict lay on the pavement to block the bus. A mob of fifty people surrounded the bus, screaming epithets like "Dirty communists!" and "Sieg Heil" while wielding bats, metal pipes, and chains. They smashed windows, slashed tires, and pounded bus walls with crowbars for twenty minutes of sheer terror before the police arrived. Despite the broken windows and pounded bus sides, the police saw no need to enforce the law. Instead, a police car escorted the bus to the city limits outside the police's jurisdiction where the terrified passengers were left with the rabid mob in a more remote area.

Out for a Sunday lynching, one teenager smashed his crowbar through one of the windows while a second hurled a homemade flaming bundle of rags through the broken window that exploded inside the bus. Passenger Genevieve Hughes was heard yelling, "Oh, my God, they're going to burn us up!" As passengers tried to breathe by pushing their heads out of the windows, people in the mob outside the bus screamed "Burn them alive!" and "fry the goddamn niggers!" When a passenger tried to leave the burning bus through the front door, he was struck in the head with a baseball bat.[7] Only an exploding fuel tank forced the mob to retreat. When a second fuel tank erupted and a passenger waved his pistol at the mob, the assaulters were kept at bay until highway patrolmen finally arrived. Police fired warning shots into the air, and the lynch mob frenzy subsided. But no police official showed any interest in arresting anyone in the mob.

An hour later, the second bus pulled into Anniston and didn't fare much better. Eight Klansmen boarded and beat the Freedom Riders mercilessly. The white community showed little empathy for the assaulted passengers. Ambulance drivers refused to transport the injured to the hospital. Klansmen blocked their entrance to the emergency room when they finally showed up. Doctors were nowhere to be found when they entered the emergency room. Fearing the mob would burn the hospital to the ground, the hospital superintendent ordered the untreated riders to leave the facility immediately. With no police protection and nightfall arriving, only the local black church deacons, pointing their shotguns at the mob, were able to hold them back long enough for the Freedom Riders to escape and continue on to Birmingham.[8]

As the two buses limped to their next destination, another mob armed with baseball bats, bicycle chains, and iron pipes assailed them again. White Freedom Riders were especially singled out. James Peck had practiced nonviolent resistance during World War II and was the only person on the Freedom Ride who had participated in an earlier Freedom Ride in 1947. He was a white

---

7 This Freedom Ride account draws on the excellent account of Raymond Arsenault, Freedom Riders: 1961 and the Struggle for Racial Justice. Gr. Brit: Oxford University Press, 2011.

8 Ibid.

civil rights hero who required more than fifty head stitches in Alabama but the medical staff at the Carraway Methodist Medical Center refused to treat him.[9]

With police supporting mob violence and mobs passionate to lynch civil rights activists, one might think the Freedom Riders would throw in the towel but no one did. Despite the shocking police collaboration with the surreal mob assaults, the protesters remained resolute as they continued into Mississippi. With courageous activists standing up to hateful racists, the whole nation was riveted on the drama. The specter of burning buses and brutal beatings forced U.S. Attorney General Robert Kennedy to dispatch aides to the area and arrange escorts for the Freedom Riders to Montgomery. National media coverage, however, also fired up white southern mob anger all the more. Lynch mobs waited along the highway where the Freedom Riders traveled. When the two drivers learned that a mob was waiting for them at the Montgomery terminal, they refused to drive to the terminal.

For the civil rights movement, these Freedom Riders were heroes. With their arrival in Montgomery, Ralph Abernathy's First Baptist Church honored them. Dr. Martin Luther King, Jr. had recently moved to the area, and spoke to the 1,500 people gathered in the church as well. Outside, a large mob taunted and attacked people who tried to attend the event. When a hopelessly inadequate contingent of U.S. Marshals was dispatched to protect the church from the white mob, city and state police sat on their hands and refused to intervene. President Kennedy called the state's governor to demand protection or face federal troop intervention. The governor reluctantly called out the National Guard, which arrived at the speed of molasses the following morning and the congregation trapped all night in the church was finally escorted out of the area.

These Freedom Riders were not making their last stand either—they were just the beginning. Successive waves kept entering the South, demanding the right to ride public buses without discrimination or violence. Each bus was met by more white mobs, who openly declared they were ready to die for their hateful cause. In state after state, more arrests and more beatings awaited the Freedom Riders.

9 Ibid.

The Kennedy administration brought intense pressure on Greyhound to provide more drivers and the U.S. Attorney General put additional pressure on the Alabama governor to shield the Freedom Ride from KKK-inspired mobs. As the Freedom Rides resumed, the next bus ride was protected by the Alabama State Highway Patrol—to a point. When it arrived at the Montgomery city limits and headed toward the South Court Street station, a lynch mob armed with baseball bats and iron pipes was waiting. The local police quietly faded away so the Freedom Riders could be beaten bloody again. Reporters and news photographers were especially singled out. Even a Justice Department official was brutally beaten and left lying on the road unconscious. Local ambulance drivers continued to refuse transportation for the injured, but the Freedom Riders continued their journey to Montgomery all the same.[10]

Behind the scenes, a desperate Kennedy administration entered into an unholy alliance with the governors of Alabama and Mississippi. State police and the National Guard agreed to protect the Freedom Riders in exchange for the federal government agreeing not to interfere with local police arresting passengers for violating local segregation ordinances. As more buses headed for Mississippi on May 24, they were escorted and protected by the Highway Patrol but when they arrived at a station, passengers could be "legally" arrested for using white-only facilities. The compromise—drawn up by federal, state, and local governments under intense public pressure—became the new government policy. Freedom Riders could travel to Mississippi without being lynched, but would be arrested when they entered a public bus terminal.

Of course, the movement would have none of that. Instead, defiant Freedom Ride volunteers flooded the Jackson and Hinds County jails to overflowing. To deal with the crisis of prison overcrowding, the Mississippi governor decided to jail Freedom Riders in the infamous Mississippi State Penitentiary, notorious for its harsh treatment of prisoners. The arrested activists would be locked up in the Mississippi Death Row maximum security unit, denied exercise and mail and issued underwear only. That's when the Movement took charge. From the dark and dreary cells of the dreaded Mississippi penitentiary, the joyful, passionate singing voices of jailed protesters filled the dungeon, morning to night, with the movement song, "We Shall Overcome."

10 Ibid.

"We Shall Overcome" was introduced to the movement by Pete Seeger and Joan Baez at folk festivals and concerts. Since neither threats nor punishment were about to deter the new inmates of the Mississippi penitentiary from their ever more beautiful exultations, the prison choir grew into many hundreds of people who took more and more buses into Mississippi, where they got to join the growing Mississippi singing celebration.[11]

Today's movement will evolve and grow like we did in the Sixties. When the courage of a massive nonviolent resistance goes on full public display from the cells of a state penitentiary, national attention finds it hard to ignore thousands of singing people whose cause is just when they refuse to back down.

These early-stage Freedom Rides paved the way for the larger mobilizations that followed, including the 1963 March on Washington and the 1964 Mississippi Freedom Summer. John Lewis spoke at the Washington gathering where Dr. Martin Luther King, Jr. delivered his "I Have a Dream" speech but it was John's courage with six hundred defiant marchers crossing a bridge in Selma, Alabama that is especially remembered today. Mounted troops brutally beat the protesters with their swinging night sticks. John's head wounds are visible today from that Selma police attack decades ago.

This is how our first wave began. Starting in the South, the freedom movement gathered momentum just like a snowball down the mountain. Students in the North mobilized as well. With each new act of resistance and each new story of courage, people sitting on the fence joined in.

Students ask me today how we were able to mobilize a mass movement with no Internet, emails, Facebook, Twitter or social media tools. Since today's social media was not yet invented, a student gathering in the early Sixties relied on volunteers cranking mimeograph machines that printed out "position papers" or leaflets. We had phones and traveled by car or bus but we lacked today's social media technologies. It hardly mattered. Our conferences were packed to overflowing. Our movement kept picking up steam. With no text messaging, the student movement spread like wildfire throughout the country.

---

11 The song "We Shall Overcome" was written by Charles Albert Tindley in 1947. It was originally called "I'll Overcome Someday." Credit goes to Zilphia Horton, who taught the lyrics to many people, including Pete Seeger.

If we could catch on fire without the power of social media, think how easy it will be for a new generation to mobilize millions of Millennials when Millennials and Generation Z awaken to change the world today.

When SDS decided to expand the Civil Rights Movement in the South into the North, we decided to support blacks, whites, and Latinos who were economically disenfranchised. To explore the possibility, we formed a project called the Economic Research and Action Project (ERAP) and I served as its first director. In the summer of 1964, one hundred and fifty students moved into ten northern cities including poor white neighborhoods in Chicago and Cleveland. SNCC had emphasized community organizing of disenfranchised blacks in the South and we wanted to organize poor blacks, poor whites and poor Latinos in the North.

I moved to Uptown Chicago where my new neighbors were mostly recent arrivals from Kentucky, West Virginia, Tennessee, Louisiana, and Alabama. We decided to invite the white working poor of Uptown to join a community union that could empower welfare mothers who had no voice in welfare offices. We were forty student organizers supporting tenants living in run-down slums and unemployed teenagers facing police brutality. We learned it takes grit and determination to organize a community that is not predisposed to join a movement. We also faced an intense opposition of a local government controlled by an entrenched political machine.

The city of Chicago was ruled by Richard Joseph Daley who had lived his whole life in an Irish American Bridgeport neighborhood on Chicago's South Side. Chicago's last political boss and its unchallenged mayor from 1955 to 1976, Daley was respected and feared for his heavy hand in city politics. He was tolerant of graft and corruption but intolerant of dissent and community organizing. Many of his top aides were convicted of corruption but Daley was never formally charged. I moved to Chicago having little idea of what it meant to organize a disenfranchised community in Mayor Daley's one-party town. I found out, however—and it was not what I expected either.

We were community organizers in our twenties living in Chicago. I spent my first night camped out on the floor of an Uptown apartment with 40 friends. Excited to begin our new adventure, but exhausted from our move, we were soundly sleeping when the apartment door blew open and uniformed Chicago police rushed in. Rudely awakened with a pistol to my head, I was shoved, half-dressed, out of the apartment into a police paddy wagon. It was the next morning before I learned why we were arrested. The front page of the Chicago Tribune described "the reason." We were throwing a drug and alcohol party that "disturbed the peace." Mayor Daley let us know our first night in Chicago that it was not our snoring that disturbed the peace but our intention to organize Uptown's poor white community. He definitely made it clear we were not welcomed in his Windy City.

I learned a lesson that night too. Before moving into a community, organizers should cultivate the media and spend time in the community getting to know the residents. Any news story that develops about the organizers should have inquiring reporters willing to investigate what actually happened before publishing the mayor's version of "the facts." The good news is that none of us felt intimidated by Daley's police raid or took his invitation to go back to where we came from seriously. Instead, we learned our lesson and went to work creating friends and allies in the community and the press. The next time we were in the media, we had media supporters. We had welfare mothers picketing welfare offices, low-income renters conducting powerful rent strikes, and teenagers bravely marching outside the local police station with picket signs demanding an end to police brutality too.

As neighborhood support for the Uptown community union called JOIN grew, Chicago police stormed us again. This time they destroyed our community center. While no one was arrested on this raid, our furniture was splintered and a large picture window shattered. I found it humorous walking through the debris imagining uniformed police beating coffee mugs into tiny pieces with their batons in the dead of the night. With the community increasingly behind us, this time we had Chicago reporters who no longer took City Hall's version of events as gospel and wanted to carry the story of what actually happened.

It was during this time that I first met Dr. Martin Luther King, Jr. He came to the city to organize open housing marches in the white working area of Cicero. He knew he would be facing hostility from the segregated community but didn't know we could bring white welfare mothers from Alabama and slum tenants from Mississippi to join him in Cicero. I decided to share the news with

Dr. King at a South Side church's men's room. As we stood side by side at two urinals, he seemed genuinely perplexed trying to comprehend my claim that poor whites who had recently moved from southern states to Chicago would participate in an open housing march led by Dr. King. White farmers and urban gang high school "hillbilly" dropouts were going to join his Chicago march against racially-segregated housing? I was kidding, right? As we spoke and laughed in the men's room, I assured him he would definitely get his hair blown back by the good people of Uptown. When hateful words and bricks went flying from the white neighborhood mobs in Cicero, our Uptown community did not disappoint my men's room bragging either.

While SDS was setting up its first urban organizing project in the North, a parallel effort was underway that summer in rural Mississippi. Organized by the Council of Federal Organizations, dozens of Freedom Schools, Freedom Houses, and community centers were preparing to register black voters in Mississippi. SNCC Field Secretary Robert Moses, who served as the project coordinator, was a civil rights activist with a master's degree in philosophy from Harvard University. He had previously taught algebra to minority students at the Horace Mann School in the Bronx. He joined the Movement in 1960 as a SNCC field secretary and later traveled to Amite County, Mississippi where blacks were a majority of the population, but completely shut out of the political process by the 1890 Mississippi constitution. Only one Afro-American was registered to vote in the entire black population. For suggesting that practice was unconstitutional, Bob Moses himself was beaten and arrested. Officials were dumbfounded when he responded by filing charges against his attacker. When the white jury acquitted the assailant, the judge made it clear that no official in the county could protect Moses for such behavior.

Amite County's name was derived from the French word for "friendship." The county seat was called "Liberty." For local black residents, friendship and liberty meant poll taxes, white bigotry and black lynchings simply because they were black and lived there.

While today's movement routinely experiences a culture of police brutality that continues to assault the black community, some of us from the Sixties vividly remember the summer of 1964. It was a time when hooded Klansmen with burning crosses felt emboldened to murder anyone, black or white, who supported racial equality or universal voting rights. With the first announcement of Freedom Summer, the White Knights of Mississippi galvanized themselves to destroy this black voter registration campaign by any means necessary.

That's the reason Bob Moses set up the 1964 Mississippi Freedom Summer in Amite County in the first place. Start in the darkest corner of the land where no other place in the country had a higher percentage of eligible black voters unable to register. With a coalition of national and regional organizations that included the NAACP and the National Council of Churches, the Mississippi project began by holding a parallel election called the Freedom Ballot to show the whole country that black Mississippi had a deep desire to vote.

Freedom Summer was launched on June 21, 1964—the same day three summer volunteers were arrested by a Neshoba County deputy sheriff. James Chaney (a black CORE activist from Mississippi), Andrew Goodman (a summer volunteer), and Michael Schwerner (a CORE organizer) were taken to jail on the opening day of the Mississippi project but released when the sun went down. As they drove away in their Ford station wagon, they were ambushed on the open road. Goodman and Schwerner were shot at point-blank range while Chaney was chased down and brutally beaten before being shot three times. Witnesses said one of the killers asked the victims, "Are you that nigger lover?" before shooting Goodman and Schwerner. Their bodies were found in a nearby earth dam on August 4, 1964. News of their murder traumatized the country and generated massive media attention for the rest of that summer.[12]

Slowly but surely, the FBI did investigate the three murders, but only because President Lyndon Johnson threatened political reprisal against FBI director Herbert Hoover if he didn't do his job. During the FBI's search for the bodies, a half-dozen other Mississippi blacks were also found. Disappearances never previously reported were discovered by the FBI.

That investigation resulted in twenty-one Mississippi men being charged with engineering a conspiracy to murder the three civil rights workers. Most of the indicted were apprehended December

12 The salient events of Freedom Summer are described in Wikipedia, the free encyclopedia. See https://en.wikipedia.org/wiki/Freedom_Summer

4, 1964, and ten were formally charged with the actual murders. Amite County's Deputy Sheriff Cecil Price played a central role as the officer who initially arrested Chaney, Goodman, and Schwerner. He was the official who released them into the night, only to chase them down himself and bring them to a remote area of Rock Cut Road where a group of white Klansmen murdered them. Everyone involved in murdering these young civil rights workers was known in the local area too. They were business owners, church leaders, "peace officers" and prominent members of the White Knights—all proud defenders of the white racist customs of Mississippi. The owner of the Old Jolly Farm where the three volunteers were buried was overheard bragging, "I've got a dam big enough to hold a hundred of them."[13] Because Mississippi state officials refused to prosecute the killers, the federal government charged the men under 18 U.S.C. §242 and §371 with conspiring to deprive the three volunteers of their civil rights by murder. Sheriff Lawrence Rainey and Deputy Sheriff Price were among the men indicted.

On October 20, 1967, Deputy Sheriff Cecil Price, Klan Imperial Wizard Samuel Bowers, Alton Wayne Roberts, Jimmy Snowden, Billy Wayne Posey, Horace Barnett, and Jimmy Arledge were found guilty. Prison sentences ranged from three to ten years, but no one served more than six. Sheriff Rainey was acquitted. The jury for Edgar Ray Killen, the local minister who was strongly implicated by several witnesses, was deadlocked because one juror said she could never convict a preacher. Every media

---

13 While everyone involved in the murder of these civil rights activists, indicted or unindicted, may have believed that Mississippi would be proud to let the "outside agitators" know where their state stood on the glory of the Confederacy, people living in Mississippi today insist they have moved on. On the twenty-fifth anniversary of the three murders, however, when the U.S. Congress passed a non-binding resolution honoring the three murdered civil rights activists, Senator Trent Lott and every other member of the Mississippi delegation refused to support the resolution. Many who live in Mississippi today have rejected this dark history. One prominent journalist—Jerry Mitchell—an investigative reporter for the *Jackson Clarion-Ledger*—helped secure convictions in other civil rights murder cases, including the murders of Medgar Evers, Vernon Dahmer, and the Birmingham Church Bombing. As a result of Mitchell's investigation, along with the exceptional work of Mississippi high school students, a multi-ethnic group of 1,500 Mississippi citizens, including Mississippi Governor Haley Barbour, called for a new inquiry into the three murders on their fortieth anniversary. On January 6, 2005, a Neshoba County grand jury indicted the minister, Edgar Ray Killen, on three counts of murder. For the first time, Mississippi itself took action. A jury convicted Killen on three counts of manslaughter. As the individual who had planned and directed the killing of the three civil rights workers, Killen was sentenced to three consecutive terms of twenty years in prison when he was eighty years old. His subsequent appeal was rejected by the Mississippi Supreme Court in 2007.

outlet covered the story and President Johnson met with the parents of Goodman and Schwerner in the White House. The massive public outrage helped push the Civil Rights Act of 1964 and the Voting Rights Act of 1965 into becoming groundbreaking national legislation. When Mississippi's legislature tried to dilute the legislation with more state legislation, the Supreme Court successfully pushed back hard.

Freedom Summer created the conditions for the 1980s and 1990s when the election of more black officials occurred in Mississippi than any other state in the union.

Pure and simple, Freedom Summer was a revolution. As the Mississippi Freedom Schools introduced subjects that had been avoided by every public school up to that time—black history and constitutional rights, for example—young children began joining their parents and grandparents in this civil rights revolution. More than 3,500 students attended Freedom Schools that summer. Volunteer teachers came to Mississippi from every state. This was a revolution that took place in church basements and front porch swings. This was a revolution where voter literacy was taught and political organizational skills were learned. Teachers were impacted as much as the students. When teacher Pam Parker wrote to her parents, she said:

> It is what every teacher dreams about—real, honest enthusiasm and desire to learn anything and everything. The girls come to class of their own free will. They respond to everything that is said. They are excited about learning. They drain me of everything that I have to offer so that I go home at night completely exhausted but very happy in spirit.[14]

In another letter, she wrote:

> Every class is beautiful. The girls respond, respond, respond. And they disagree among themselves. I have no doubt that soon they will be disagreeing with me. At least this is one thing that I am working towards. They are a sharp group. But they are undereducated and starved for knowledge. They know that they have been cheated and they want anything

---

14 Allen, Chude Pam Parker. "Three Letters from a Freedom School Teacher." Holly Springs, Mississippi, July 1964.

> and everything that we can give them. I feel inadequate to the task of teaching them but I keep saying to myself that as long as I continue to feel humble there is a chance that we might all learn a whole lot together.[15]

As the Sixties Movement took shape, its organizers were solid and unwavering—always taking the high moral standard of nonviolence. One of history's powerful concepts, civil resistance and nonviolence were the cornerstone of the India movement led by Mahatma Gandhi to end British rule. Dr. Martin Luther King, Jr. put his nonviolent stake in the ground as well and never budged an inch when facing the pressures of hateful southern mobs. Cesar Chavez opposed the brutal treatment of California farm workers with a philosophy of nonviolence too. When the Czechoslovakian nation overthrew its communist government, it was a nonviolent revolution as well. In his book *Stride Toward Freedom*, Dr. King urged the Civil Rights Movement to adopt nonviolence as its way of life. The mission of nonviolence, King said, is to defeat injustice, not people. In King's famous "Letter from Birmingham Jail," he encouraged the Civil Rights Movement to become experts on its opponents' position. For Dr. King, a movement should resort to direct action only when a person or institution was no longer willing to enter into discussion. For Dr. King, nonviolence was not about weakness. It took strength, courage and wisdom to stay nonviolent when confronted by police brutality or a violent mob. A nonviolence strategy delivered a powerful moral pressure to resolve an entrenched injustice.[16]

As the first wave of today's movement galvanizes, is nonviolence still relevant? Nonviolence is how an early stage movement connects to the public. For Millennials who will lead today's movement, it is essential to understand and realize that breaking windows and looting businesses to change the world will destroy a movement. There is nothing wrong with common sense guiding an emerging movement to change the world.

Looking back on the Sixties movement, we built our power by staying nonviolent. We lost support when some in our movement forgot and lost their way.

---

15 Ibid.

16 King, Jr., Martin Luther. "Letter from Birmingham Jail." *Why We Can't Wait*. New York: Penguin Books, 1963.

We have to step out of the box of conventional society to pioneer a movement. We must never forget that no government conceived of the Sixties revolution and no congress or parliament paved our way. When the federal government was powerless to enforce its own laws, it was regular people, many in their twenties, who courageously put themselves inside a rural Mississippi culture and drew a line in the sand. After two centuries of brutal white supremacy fueling intense hatred and bigotry towards the black community of the United States, the Sixties Movement declared America's racism must end. The Democratic Party followed our movement, not the other way around. It was our movement that declared the violence of one group against another must stop. "We Shall Overcome" were no longer the words of a church gospel but the heart felt creed of a Movement determined to change the world.

The Sixties movement set out to change a bigoted culture of hate that had its roots in the founding of a nation. Racism continued for a century into a brutal civil war. It was a culture of fear and divide that pledged to never examine itself. When white mobs and black lynchings could not be stopped by either political party a century after the Civil War—or by any local, state, or federal officials—the Sixties movement did what no government or political party could do on its own.

We stood down the entrenched racist culture that brazenly claimed one race had the right to enslave another. Confronting and changing what no government could imagine was how our Movement began.

For people who support Black Lives Matter in the present time, what we started in the Sixties can be finished today. The courage to organize massive civil disobedience will develop with training, inspiration and time.

A movement may start off standing up for real justice in local communities but it can build over time into national platforms that change the root causes of racism and police brutality. Governments get pushed by avalanches. Trump's Attorney General will feel the heat when fifty thousand people surrounding the Justice Department are willing to sit in the streets and be arrested.

What can today's movement learn from the Sixties movement?

Be brave. Stop being a goody two shoes. Dare to change the root causes. Leave society and stand up for humanity. Feel your passion. Trust yourself. Let your wild side come out and don't be afraid. You are not a tiny, insignificant voice any more . You are a movement. You are an avalanche that takes out walls.

Chapter 3

DISCOVERING VIETNAM

Seeing the War with My Own Eyes

I welcomed the Civil Rights Act (1964) and the Voting Rights Act (1965), but felt there was little time to stop and celebrate the new legislation. Racism remained a dominant American reality and the U.S. military was stepping up its war in Southeast Asia as well. As U.S. troop levels soared from 3,500 Marines, initially deployed for "defense" to 450,000 "boots on the ground," our Movement knew we had to keep moving—so we did. Going forward, we discovered there was a national audience for ending the war in Vietnam. By building our support with the public, we became the largest antiwar and civil rights movement in American history.

Today, the Sixties Movement is an historic memory. Some of our institutions would like to see that history fade into oblivion. War has been a part of the American psyche for so long that governments seem to prefer that the public forget that the United States once mobilized a massive antiwar movement that reflected the majority of our public opinion. The Sixties movement is the part of our history that challenges America's official self-image. To understand this extraordinary historical antiwar phenomenon, 1967 seems a good place to start.

That year, the U.S. government was conducting 2,000 bombing sorties on North and South Vietnam weekly. The total ordnance that rained down in 1967 alone was 1.5 million tons of explosives, a nearly inconceivable destruction that grew to 8 million tons by the war's end, making an area the size of New Mexico the most bombed nation on Earth. That same year, the U.S. military was defoliating 1.7

Fourth Generation

Chemical Agent Orange Victim

million acres in South Vietnam with chemical Agent Orange, pursuing a policy of "clearing the jungles"—a war crime that eventually caused genetic mutations, birth defects, and environmental ruin for future Vietnamese generations. The United States government does not want to be charged with war crimes but four decades after signing the Paris Peace Accords in Paris to end the war, cleanup of the U.S. contamination has been limited to three U.S. military bases where the chemicals were stored. The toxic U.S. poison is still in Vietnam's ponds and lakes today. Drinking the water or consuming the fish in contaminated areas can result in sickness or death in the present time. We can pretend chemical Agent Orange never happened but that doesn't explain the three million Vietnamese disabled from Agent Orange today. The year this book was published, 300,000 Vietnamese were born deformed because chemical Agent Orange was sprayed on their grandparents, who passed their genetic affliction to a fourth generation. We rarely see a news story about this tragedy, now that the Vietnam War is over and the U.S. antiwar movement is our forgotten history. Fortunately, today's movement to change the world does not need to forget what the U.S. government did in Vietnam decades ago.

The national media today is a constant source of news for the Trump resistance movement. During the Vietnam war, the public learned about the Vietnam War through a new type of reporting as well. Reporters weren't "embedded" in military units like they are today. They could travel on their own or catch a military helicopter ride into a hot war zone. During the Vietnam War, the message of our movement was broadcast into American living rooms coast to coast every night. As the facts of the war were reported, antiwar sentiment grew by leaps and bounds. By April, 1967, Dr. Martin Luther King, Jr. was ready to lend his considerable weight to the antiwar movement by speaking to 400,000 people against the war in New York City.

The war in Vietnam caused our movement to grow swiftly as the diverse organizations against the war began to unite. Today, we have many organizations working for change but no coalition that ties us all together. Climate change is coming, however. Like the war in Vietnam, climate change will initially come into our lives through television as well. But climate change will also show up in our pocketbooks, drought experiences, dying oceans, mass migrations and the alarming worldwide water shortages.

Today's movement will also find a way to unite hundreds of diverse organizations into networks and coalitions.

In the late Sixties, we created a coalition of 150 national organizations that committed themselves to work together on two transcending issues—end the U.S. war in Vietnam and end America's entrenched racial discrimination. Today's movement faces a new set of conditions that will cause our diverse groups to unite as well. Coalition building is hard but it brings a sea change for a movement that wants to change the world.

As the antiwar movement grew in size and influence, we were able to awaken the sleeping giant of the public. By 1967, a majority of American voters, according to opinion polls, supported the Vietnam War. By late 1968, opinion polls showed a majority of American voters supported our position to end the war and bring our GIs home. Having a coalition was one of the reasons the Sixties movement made this great leap forward—and the nightmare of the Republican Party favors the same development in the present time as well.

In 1967, I wanted to learn more about the war in Vietnam and felt excited when a daring invitation was made toward the middle of that year. An American delegation was invited to meet with a high level delegation of Vietnamese at a conference in Bratislava, Czechoslovakia. While I believed the undeclared war was morally and politically wrong, I had a superficial understanding of Vietnam's history, especially its tradition of defeating one military invader after another. The countries defeated by Vietnam ranged from Mongolia in the 13th century to modern nations like France and Japan. I did not consider myself particularly "pro-Vietnam" but believed our State Department should stop eroding our democratic principles with its refusal to allow elections that would let Vietnam determine its own direction. I did not believe an economically poor, Third World country could actually defeat the world's leading military superpower. In 1967, that concept seemed inconceivable. I only knew I wanted to learn more about this tiny Southeast Asian country.

Had my parents known I was flying to Czechoslovakia to attend a conference "with the enemy," they would have done their best to dissuade me. For them, this was risky business. Being labeled unpatriotic by the House Un-American Activities Committee was the worst thing possible to them. It didn't particularly intimidate me. In fact, I rather relished the idea that I could poke some fun at Congress for its reckless witch hunt absurdities—an opportunity that would come to me later. For my parents, however, it was unwise to travel to a Warsaw Pact nation and meet with representatives of a country with which the U.S. government was at war. My parents' viewpoint was mainstream thinking too, reflecting a long American tradition that we had to support our government in times of war. Opposition to any U.S. war was equated with aiding the enemy. When our movement decided to call out this tradition, we saw nothing wrong in opposing our government by standing up for our nation's ideals when it was our own country that had rejected the international Geneva Agreement with its provisions for democratic elections after the Vietnamese defeat of the French. Pointing that out in public didn't mean we were unpatriotic. For the Sixties movement, patriotism meant supporting our soldiers. Supporting our soldiers meant bringing them home from a war that was legally flawed and morally unjust.

In previous American wars, the public united against "the enemy." During the Vietnam War, our Movement figured it out. We realized Vietnam was not our enemy.

The Sixties movement dared to challenge the historic patriotism of "my country, right or wrong". We decided not to deny war crimes when they were carried out by our own government. To us, supporting our country to become a better nation was a breath of fresh air. A massive public movement opposing war crimes in Vietnam was not a dishonor to our values but a proud milestone for America.

Once upon a time not so long ago, millions of Americans opposed a ruinous war in which our government had propped up a brutal South Vietnamese dictator who rejected democratic elections. It was a time when our own State Department supported Saigon prison torture camps built to crush the dictator's opposition. It was also a time when millions of Americans said no. It took time for us to build a viable national opposition against the war but we did and the American public eventually shifted their opinion and agreed with us.

Vietnam

Douglas Hostetter Photos

Even Robert McNamara, the U.S. Secretary of Defense who directed the war in Vietnam during Johnson's term, eventually decided he could denounce the policies he once managed and improve his public image.

Opposing the Vietnam War wasn't an act of treason. I certainly thought of myself as a patriot when I became one of the forty-two Americans to meet the leaders of the Vietnamese resistance. We were a cross-section of antiwar, civil rights, and women activists with a handful of journalists. Martin Luther King, Jr. was invited as well but declined at the last moment due to a scheduling conflict. We flew to Paris and then to Prague before taking a bus to Bratislava where we met twenty-three Vietnamese, including members of the Vietnamese national assembly and ranking leaders of South Vietnam's Provisional Revolutionary Government.

I slowly realized that the Vietnam delegation was the highest level gathering of officials to meet outside of Vietnam since the Geneva Convention in 1954—the historic conference that ended the Indochina War between France and the Vietminh in a settlement that split French Indochina into three countries—Vietnam, Laos, and Cambodia. In that international conference, Vietnam was provisionally partitioned along the seventeenth parallel, pending a countrywide election in 1956 to unify the country and choose a new national leadership. With direction from the U.S. government, however, the South Vietnamese President Ngo Dinh Diem rejected the international agreement, knowing full well that the Vietnamese population would overwhelmingly support the popular Vietnamese resistance leader, Ho Chi Minh, in any free and fair election.

Arriving in Bratislava, I met Madam Nguyen Thi Binh for the first time. She greeted us warmly in her elegant full-length, high-collared Vietnamese dress known as *ao dai*. In a few short years, she would become a public sensation as the elegant, articulate, and stunning head of the South Vietnamese "Viet Cong" delegation—one of the four parties to the U.S-Vietnam peace accord held in Paris. When the Vietnam War ended, Madam Binh became the Vice President of a unified country for two terms.

At the time, however, the American public had a blurry and distorted image of Vietnam's resistance leaders. They were perceived as shadowy, vicious, jungle-fighting guerrillas. When their official representative in Paris was the enchanting and elegant Madam Nguyen Thi Binh, the American public felt confused. When she stepped onto the world stage on November 4, 1968—a wise, sensitive, and articulate spokeswoman—she stunned the whole world. As hundreds of delegations made their journey to Paris to meet her, she won many hearts and minds with her kindness and patient explanations of the deeply-flawed, brutal American war policy.

Madam Nguyen Thi Binh
Wikepedia Photo

Growing up, Madam Binh lived with her family on a boat and attended a French school in Cambodia. In April, 1951, however, her education was abruptly halted when she was seized and imprisoned by the French. She spent three years in the most notorious French prison of the time after someone who had been brutally tortured gave up her name. She writes about her torture in her autobiography:

> I was cruelly beaten without stopping because an earlier arrestee had broken down under torture and given my name. First, they tortured us by savage beatings. Then they submerged us in water, then with electricity, then—I wanted to die so they would finish—I was most worried about

> breaking under torture and giving names, leading the enemy to arrest others...[17]

In recalling those brutal years, Madam Binh said it gave her the strength "to survive the most intense conditions imaginable."[18]

American reporters wondered why Madam Binh was selected for Vietnam's key Paris assignment. The simple answer was Ho Chi Minh. The president of Vietnam had previously lived in New York City and Boston during the women's suffrage movement before World War I. Those experiences motivated him to embrace the idea that a woman should represent Vietnam to the world and he knew Madam Binh possessed the intelligence, openness, and kindness to win over the public including the skeptics.

In Bratislava, our American delegation knew nothing of this. Having flown across the Atlantic Ocean, we entered the hotel like a ragtag, jetlagged collection of disheveled American tourists. When we first met the members of the Vietnamese delegation, they were refreshed and elegantly dressed. It took days for me to comprehend the months of travel, risks, and hardship the delegation from the South underwent to make this trip. But on that first evening, they fussed over us like parents care for their children, making sure we were comfortable and settled in.

Throughout the weeklong conference, formal and informal discussions ranged from presentations about Vietnam's history to the complex military challenges surrounding the conflict with the United States. I was relieved when the sessions lacked the feel of bureaucratic stiffness or tightly scripted propaganda, although the translators sometimes struggled to keep up. All the Vietnamese were approachable and their passion for their country seemed genuine. Steeped in the realities of their own amazing history, they talked about centuries of war like it was yesterday. They were living participants in a two-thousand-year epic and understood how citizens from the invading country would slowly oppose their country's invasion. It happened during a thirty-year Mongol-Vietnamese War in the thirteenth century and occurred again when public opinion in France turned against that government's invasion of Vietnam. With the humiliating defeat of French troops by Vietnamese forces at Dien Bien Phu,

---

17 Binh, Madam Nguyen Thi. *Family, Friends, and Country, Autobiography*. Tri Thuc Publishing House, 2013. p. 51-2.

18 Ibid. p. 78.

the French public felt exhausted and eager to end the Vietnam war. This historic pattern of public opposition to a Vietnam War was starting to emerge in the United States as well.

While U.S. military strategists appeared oblivious to this history, the Vietnamese drew strength from these centuries of experience and seemed certain an antiwar movement would emerge in the United States—which it did.

I could have left Bratislava with a richer understanding of Vietnam. I could have come back to America more educated about their history. But something unexpected happened, causing my Vietnam experience to shift from educated and informed to up close and personal. At the close of the conference, I was invited with six other Americans to visit Vietnam and see for myself what I had heard at the conference. I was stunned by the invitation and wanted to see Vietnam with my own eyes. Every American invited felt the same. As risky as traveling to Czechoslovakia may have been, there was no comparison with the potential consequences of an unsanctioned trip into "enemy" territory. While I never considered declining the invitation, I found it hard to evaluate the risks. Would I be bombed by U.S. Navy warplanes stationed on carriers offshore Vietnam? Would I be vilified by the press returning home? Believing America had strayed from its core principles, I felt motivated to be among the first Americans to evaluate the Vietnamese claim that American air raids targeted civilian populations—an assertion vigorously rejected by our Pentagon. The official—and frequently repeated—Pentagon claim was that the U.S. bombing campaign sought to destroy military targets only. By traveling "behind enemy lines" I could become a type of citizen reporter, investigating whether deception of the public by our own government was or was not taking place.

I knew this trip could have potential consequences for my father too. He had served as the Chief of Staff of Truman's Council of Economic Advisors before joining a government team creating strategies for the unthinkable event of nuclear war. A few miles from our Virginia farm, some of the hardest rock in America had become a favorite place for testing drill bits. That mine eventually became an underground bunker that housed large-scale government functions in the event of a nuclear war. My dad was prominent in the field of labor productivity, and was recruited to develop labor scenarios should there be a nuclear exchange.

He wasn't allowed to talk about his work, but I learned a little here and there over the years. I learned he was the "Secretary of Labor" in a stand-in government should nuclear war destroy the United States. I learned he worked at Mt. Weather that had its own intelligence gathering capacity. I learned how one afternoon he was visited by that security wing and bluntly asked whether he was aware I was about to board a plane in Vientiane, Laos for Hanoi. That had to be one awkward moment for him.

When the invitation to visit Hanoi came from the Vietnamese delegation, I pondered long and hard about calling my family to share the news. Our home phone was part of a rural party line, and our phone number was 174J12. We never dialed a number. We just picked up the receiver and got an operator. I laugh, remembering it now. When our home phone rang—one long ring followed by two short rings—we were supposed to pick up. Of course, when it was our ring, all our curious neighbors picked up too. While we were not a family that kept secrets from each other, I knew sharing the news of my trip to North Vietnam over that party line was a bad idea. It seemed better to tell my family when I got back. I never imagined my dad would find out anyway in the awkward way he did.

Our delegation to Hanoi (Tom Hayden, Carol McEldowney, Vivian Rothstein, Norman Fructurer, Robert Allen, Jock Brown, and myself) took seats aboard a small International Control Commission (ICC) aircraft heading into a war zone. The ICC was an offshoot of the Geneva Convention established to monitor the implementation of the Geneva Accords following the French war in 1954. When its mandate for unifying the country with nationwide elections was blocked by the United States, ICC continued to provide an airline connection to the divided country with flights from Saigon to Hanoi through Laos.

Our nighttime flight into Hanoi was the final leg of a journey that had begun in Prague and taken us through Beirut, Dubai, Bombay, Rangoon, Phnom Penh (Cambodia), and Vientiane (Laos). We faced stormy weather that night, and intense air currents hurled our tiny prop plane sharply upwards before dropping hard over and over, making passengers tightly bound to their throw-up bags. I was relieved not to feel sick as we descended into the pitch darkness of this mysterious Southeast Asian city. At the last moment, a row of bright lights marking the runway went on briefly as the wheels touched the ground. As I walked down the plane's stairs, a group of excited Vietnamese welcomed us. I got my travel bag and walked to a small caravan of jeep-style military vehicles for transport, feeling overwhelmed with questions. Were we in danger of bombs being dropped by our own country tonight? How would we get into the city if all the bridges over the Red River had been bombed? Was it okay to talk with ordinary Vietnamese, or would our visit be tightly controlled and scripted? I had my questions but didn't have to wait long for answers.

To reach Hanoi from the airport, the Red River—a major waterway flowing from Yunnan in Southwestern China to the Gulf of Tonkin—had to be crossed. The main bridge across that river was repeatedly bombed, but somehow, never destroyed. When we reached the river's edge, however, it was deemed safer by our hosts to board a ferry and cross the Red River discreetly. And yes, we could speak with the Vietnamese on board the ferry.

On this warm, humid night with a bright tropical moon casting a liquid silver glow on the water and illuminating the faces of every passenger, I could see the Vietnamese on the ferry looked friendly. In fact, they were surprisingly open. With only the sound of the boat's motor and a radio tuned to the music of a bamboo flute, all was quiet as we crossed the Red River. Surrounded by the sound of this simple elegant music and the idyllic scents, and serene sights, I felt like I had traveled back in time to some ancient century. Looking directly into the faces of the people around me, I noticed no one seemed stressed or worried at all. No one looked guarded either. By comparison, when I took a commuter train from the O'Hare International Airport into Uptown Chicago, there were always passengers who looked guarded. If I had to pick one word to describe the demeanor of these Hanoi ferry boat passengers, I would say innocent. It seems strange to say, but that was my impression. It took me by surprise too. Vietnam was being bombed daily by the United States, yet these Vietnamese seemed entirely comfortable with a group of Americans next to them. They appeared largely free of body armor, defenses, and cunning too. When the radio music was interrupted by the voice of an announcer and everyone hushed to listen, I could only watch in amazement at everyone's rapt attention to every word. Then the boat suddenly erupted with cheering and clapping. I turned to our guide to hear his translation. "It was just reported," he said, "that an F-16 flew over the country and was shot down by an eighteen-year-old woman with a rifle."

Now I was confused—and conflicted too. My immediate thoughts went to the pilot. A U.S. serviceman had been shot down by a woman's rifle, and I'm surrounded by a heart felt flood of excitement. I wasn't prepared for this surprise. As my emotions gradually settled down, I tried to stay open and let myself see how ordinary Vietnamese actually felt about this war. I saw they had a genuine passion for their country that I would repeatedly witness in the coming days. From my very first hours in Hanoi, I saw with my own eyes that the United States might not be fighting an ideology or the narrow agenda of a rigid political elite after all. None of these people seemed forced to obey government propaganda. In fact, they seemed like a perfect nation for "containing China," as our State Department stated the United States was determined to do.

Throughout the trip, I watched everyday Vietnamese demonstrate their enthusiasm for their cause of national freedom and independence. In diverse ways, they showed me this was their war, their country, and their duty to fight for their country's freedom. I started to feel like someone who had slipped into one of the American colonies from Great Britain to witness a small band of freedom fighters during our own country's war of independence. I felt like that invisible Brit who got to overhear the news of a victory won by a ragtag American army fighting for its freedom. From my first moments in Vietnam, I realized I was witnessing one of history's special examples of how ordinary people can unite to defend their independence.

Before this trip to Hanoi, it never occurred to me that the Vietnamese might actually defeat the world's greatest military power. The Vietnamese, however, seemed convinced that, in the end, they would prevail, just as they had done against the French at Dien Bien Phu, against the Japanese during World War II, and against the Chinese and Mongols to the north repeatedly over the centuries. They clearly lacked any sense of desperation one would expect from hopelessly outgunned underdogs. Instead, they displayed a confidence that made me wonder whether the war in Vietnam might be more than a misguided foreign policy for containing China. Could the United States be engaged in a foolish military strategy as well?

Over the course of my first visit to Vietnam, it became increasingly difficult to believe the official American position that Vietnamese guerrillas were Russian or Chinese pawns manipulated by foreign powers in a global game of chess. The people I met seemed like patriots. I was a believer in democracy and supported fair and open elections. I didn't like that Vietnam was a one-party government but couldn't deny the Vietnamese I met seemed genuinely motivated to preserve their nation and traditions they deeply loved.

Where I lived in Chicago, people had only a vague idea of what this war was about. Unless a person was part of a military family fighting in Vietnam, Chicago residents had little stake in the outcome. Everyone on this ferry seemed to possess a passionate stake in the outcome, no matter the costs or the time it took to win back their country. I felt sick in my stomach thinking about the American GIs in South Vietnam who had been sent to war by a government that was so clearly out of touch with this Vietnamese reality.

When we reached the old French quarter of Hanoi, I could see our hotel had once been a French colonial building and was rather drab and run-down on the outside. But it was brightened by huge displays of colorful and fragrant tropical flowers inside. In fact, flowers and delicious tropical fruits were everywhere I went in Hanoi. At times, I could hear bombs explode in parts of the city, yet the streets were a crowded maze of sidewalk merchants and food vendors with families preparing meals outdoors on the sidewalks, as pedestrians weaved precariously through speeding bicycles, motorcycles, and buses crossing intersections with no traffic lights. Most people wore traditional Vietnamese clothing, including the iconic bamboo hat symbolic of the Vietnamese peasant. Rich, exotic smells sloshed through the air like tropical punch in a bowl. In a city of contrasts and a nation at war, the famous Hoa Sua—milk flower— trees were in bloom, and our hotel was six blocks from a beautiful lake lined by clouds of silky white blossoms and ancient pagodas.

Our first days in Hanoi were a flurry of meetings like Bratislava. Our hosts had a contrary viewpoint to what the American public was told which I expected but I was always looking out for blatant propaganda—information that had a "party line" feel to it or was not in keeping with what I had witnessed myself. I saw political billboards and posters in the streets, but none displayed overt, anti-American imagery. Instead, they mostly promoted the ideal of Vietnamese heroes of all ages. A typical billboard showed a father, mother, son, and daughter with rifles on their backs and a message about freedom and independence. Everyone we met seemed genuinely appreciative that we were there, too. They openly expressed their respect for the American people and often compared the American Revolution to their own history of defending Vietnam against foreign invaders. We met women's groups where the role women played in the resistance was celebrated. We heard presentations from youth organizations that rivaled our own massive youth movement in the United States. We met with the Prime Minister. We visited a war museum that had artifacts taken from various foreign invasions dating back hundreds of years. On several occasions, we walked through bombed out buildings in civilian areas of Hanoi that defied the claims of our own Pentagon.

One evening, I was strolling down a Hanoi street with one of my hosts when we came to a large truck caravan parked and waiting. Its destination was clearly South Vietnam. I noticed many of the parked trucks had pictures on their windshields. One was President Ho Chi Minh. Another was a Western face I did not recognize. I asked several drivers through my translator who that was on their windshield next to Ho Chi Minh. "Norman Morrison" was the response. I knew the Morrison story. He was an American Quaker who, on November 2, 1965, committed suicide in an act of self-immolation at age thirty-one protesting U.S. involvement in the Vietnam War. He doused himself in kerosene and set himself on fire below Defense Secretary Robert McNamara's Pentagon office. Morrison had adopted a philosophy of sacrifice following the 1963 self-immolation of Buddhist monk Thich Quang Duc, who burned himself to death in downtown Saigon to protest the repression of the South Vietnam government. Morrison's act was not widely publicized in the United States but in Vietnam, Morrison was a hero. His sacrifice influenced U.S. Secretary of Defense, Robert McNamara, too. According to filmmaker Errol Morris, who interviewed McNamara for his documentary *The Fog of War,* McNamara told him, "[Morrison] came to the Pentagon, doused himself with gasoline. Burned himself to death below my office... his wife issued a very moving statement—'human beings must stop killing other human beings'—and that's a belief that I shared, I shared it then, I believe it even more strongly today."[19]

Americans who knew Morrison remembered him as devoutly and sincerely sacrificing himself for the Vietnam cause. In Vietnam, he was remembered in multiple ways. Vietnamese poet Tố

---

19 *The Fog of War*. Dir. Errol Morris. 2003.

Hữu wrote a poem titled, *"Emily, My Child,"* as if Morrison were speaking to his daughter Emily to tell her the reasons for his sacrifice. Vietnam named a Hanoi street after him and issued a postage stamp in his honor. Vietnamese truck drivers bound for South Vietnam displayed his picture on their windshields. Years later, when Vietnamese President Nguyễn Minh Triết visited the United States, he stopped at a site on the Potomac near where Morrison had immolated himself to read the poem by Tố Hữu to commemorate the Morrison sacrifice.

Hanoi was rooted in an ancient tradition that had been thrust into a modern war. With intense aerial bombardments, Vietnamese in Hanoi listened to bamboo music on loud speakers. Only air raid alerts interrupted the gentle music. During one alert, our delegation was hustled into the nearest bomb shelter where we sat in dark underground bunkers, feeling the ground shake as a 500-lb. bomb exploded in the city. On another occasion, we left Hanoi to visit a rural village. Our Jeep caravan was abruptly flagged down by local residents shouting the Vietnamese words "danger! danger!" Even I understood what they were saying as I was pulled from my Jeep and carried—yes, *carried*—by one of my Vietnamese hosts to the nearest "bomb shelter." It was a ditch on the side of the road. I lay on the ground as he covered me with his body. Seconds later, a U.S. fighter jet buzzed our position at very low altitude, trying to stay under the radar on its way to its bombing target.

Rural Vietnam opened my eyes. I saw young boys, old men, and women. The men were gone and Vietnam looked to the women to keep their roads open for travel which was no easy task, either.

Consider the Mark 84—an American general-purpose bomb dropped by the U.S. Air Force with a weight of 2,000 lbs. Upon explosion, it left a crater fifty feet wide and thirty-six feet deep. Some craters were larger—up to 150 feet across. A single bomb could penetrate up to eleven feet of concrete, depending on the height from which it dropped, causing lethal fragmentation to a radius of 400 yards. Filling one of those craters was a considerable task too, especially with few trucks or bulldozers available. Undeterred, thousands of women, with two baskets suspended from a bamboo pole filled with dirt precariously balanced on one shoulder, would descend on a gaping crater in the road. With utter dedication and passion, these five-foot tall

Vietnamese women would fly into action with a spirit anyone would call inspiring, no matter their viewpoint on the war. With large trucks backed up and waiting on both sides of a massive crater, they moved the dirt two baskets at a time, filling the giant hole while singing. Their passionate effort could get any road running again with a speed that was spectacular.

Visiting these rural Vietnamese villages, I learned how U.S. military strategists think about a people's war from their perspective.

In rural Vietnam, I had my first encounter with the mindset that had conceived and engineered the cluster bomb unit (CBU). Many women told me their stories about U.S. bombing raids employing this weapon. When I testified in federal court during the trial of the Chicago Seven, I held up one of the unexploded bomblets from a CBU that a Vietnamese woman had given me. It was the approximate size of a tennis ball. A large cluster bomb had released this bomblet that was now an unexploded ordnance whose canister held hundreds of these little spheres of death. When the bomblets exploded, they spewed metal shrapnel over an area the size of multiple football fields, killing or wounding people with an indiscriminate devastation. Each sphere sent out 300 pieces of jagged steel shrapnel. Peasants were decapitated. Arms, legs, hands, or feet were severed from bodies. A single piece of shrapnel could strike a leg and ricochet up through the body, leaving a pathway for a slow bleeding to death. CBUs were dropped on North Vietnam during a time when the official Department of Defense's position was that military targets only—"steel and concrete"—were the only U.S. targets. It was obvious no cluster bomb could destroy steel and concrete, but could easily kill a water buffalo or a water buffalo boy. Not banned until 2008 by the Convention on Cluster Munitions, CBUs were widely used in North Vietnam by the United States during the time I visited. That's what I saw with my own eyes.

Following my return to the United States, I spoke to our first large antiwar Pentagon mobilization in October, 1967. During this televised event, I held up that unexploded bomblet I had brought back from a Vietnamese village and described how this weapon could kill civilians, but could not destroy steel and concrete. That day, I joined 150,000 people who marched on the Pentagon and placed flowers in the rifle barrels of soldiers our own age ordered to protect the Pentagon. I returned from Vietnam to join our coalition's first large-scale anti mobilization. The year was 1967 and our anti war movement was gaining real momentum.

When a reporter interviewed me for a Chicago daily about my Vietnam trip, his report of my eyewitness account was carried in hundreds of papers by the Associated Press for three consecutive days. Reading my account—that Vietnamese civilians were bombed by U.S. pilots using 'anti-personnel' weapons—the Defense Department shot back with a sharp rebuttal, claiming I had been "brainwashed" by the North Vietnamese.

Facing my youthful belief that our government would never lie to the American public shaken, I knew it was time to share publicly what I had seen with my own eyes. I left community organizing to join America's largest anti war movement in history, unaware that my own life would never be the same.

Chapter 4

CHICAGO 1968

Police Riot and the Whole World is Watching

Hunkered down in a bomb shelter in Hanoi, I listened to an Associated Press newsfeed read out loud by our Vietnamese hosts. That's how I learned the Democratic National Convention would be held in my hometown of Chicago. Hearing the news, I knew I would somehow be involved.

1968 was a year of extraordinary anti war protests, some of them small and spontaneous, but all of them building towards one game-changing event in Chicago. The city was hosting the national convention for the Democratic Party and our Movement was hosting an anti war demonstration outside the Convention hall. The clash of positions would change American opinion about the war in Vietnam. Historians said that our protests at the Chicago Democratic National Convention were watched on television by more people than watched the first moon landing.

Before the Chicago demonstrations began, a Gallup poll reported the majority of the American public supported the government's war in Vietnam. After the demonstrations, a Gallup poll showed the American majority opposed the war in Vietnam. I won't recount all the drama and trauma that happened in Chicago since articles, books, and films about this watershed event abound, but I will share my personal experiences that I feel have relevance again as we prepare ourselves today for humanity's greatest adventure.

Lyndon B. Johnson was President of the United States when our anti war coalition started planning the Chicago demonstration. At the time, our Movement was his only serious opposition. Senator Robert F. Kennedy made it clear he would not run as a candidate for the anti-Johnson movement and other prominent Democrats refused to run against a sitting president as well. While millions of Democrats opposed the Vietnam war, anyone following the media pundits assumed President Johnson would be unopposed in Chicago. That made our Movement his only real opposition. In late 1967 and early 1968, our protests were accelerating across the country too. In October, 1967 alone, 15,000 men in eighteen cities burned or turned in their draft cards. Three thousand demonstrators blocked access to the Oakland army induction center. Another 150,000 people marched on the Pentagon. Even with our Movement building support among many voters, no Democratic leader felt able to challenge the sitting president conducting the war. My own supposition was that rank and file Democrats would join us outside the convention hall. When I first started to prepare for Chicago '68, I estimated 500,000 people would join our Chicago protest against the war in Vietnam.

Minnesota Senator Eugene J. McCarthy was the first Democrat willing to oppose Johnson's war policies and seek the Democratic nomination himself. Taking the first plunge, he stunned the nation by winning 42 percent of the vote in the first New Hampshire primary. The media declared McCarthy the "moral victor," even though Johnson had earned 49 percent. Organizations supporting McCarthy quickly sprang up, especially among college students. McCarthy's overnight political success created a youth campaign similar to the one led by Bernie Sanders. The McCarthy movement changed the political calculation and threw open the door for Robert Kennedy to enter the race as well.

On March 16, 1968, the brother of President John F. Kennedy announced he would run for president too. As surprising as that was, the nation was stunned again two weeks later when Lyndon Johnson announced he would not seek the Chicago nomination at all. On June 5, Senator Kennedy won the California primary. Then Senator George McGovern entered the race and suddenly anti-war sentiment had the support of major voices inside the Democratic Party.

During this time of shifting political sands, I was working outside the two-party system, negotiating permits for our Chicago antiwar mobilization. With the possibility that the United States might end the war through national elections, our plans were in flux too. When Mayor Daley made it known he had no intention of granting us permits or acknowledging our First Amendment right to assemble and petition, our plans had to change again. Facing the hostile environment of a city government and the emergence of several presidential antiwar candidates, we needed a backup plan. One main plan was to hold a massive public demonstration outside the Democratic Convention hall on the night of the presidential nomination. Our backup plan envisioned hundreds of mobile medics and marshals supporting a more youthful fluid turnout in a Chicago park.

The summer of 1968 was a tempestuous American crossroads that felt like an ominous storm was approaching. The public's mood was darkening too. Martin Luther King, Jr. was assassinated at the Lorraine Motel in Memphis, Tennessee that spring and riots ignited in more than 100 cities, including Chicago. Mayor Daley responded by issuing orders to his police to "shoot-to-kill" the looters.

King had made death part of his philosophy, declaring in public speeches that murder would never stop the American struggle for civil rights. He had received death threats for years and understood the American sickness for murdering its public leaders. When President John F. Kennedy was assassinated, Dr. King, in a fateful premonition, told his wife Coretta that "this is going to happen to me also."

On the day King was assassinated, Senator Robert F. Kennedy held a final campaign stop in a predominantly black area of Indianapolis. The city's police chief told Senator Kennedy he should cancel the event because the police force could not guarantee his protection. Kennedy proceeded anyway, standing on a podium mounted on a flatbed truck and delivering a moving five-minute soliloquy where the audience learned of the King assassination for the first time. While other cities rioted that night, Indianapolis did not—many believing one of the great public oratories in American history to be the reason. Kennedy's moving remarks ended by saying, "Let us dedicate ourselves to what the Greeks wrote so many years ago: 'to tame the savageness of man and make gentle the life of this world.' Let us dedicate ourselves to that and say a prayer for our country and for our people."[20]

The nation responded to King's assassination as if someone from their immediate family had been taken. President Lyndon B. Johnson declared April 7 a national day of mourning. Two days later, 300,000 people attended King's funeral as King eulogized

20 Kennedy, Robert F. *The History Place*. Great Speeches Collection, April 4, 1968.

himself with a recording from his "Drum Major" sermon given February 4 when he said he wanted no mention at his funeral of his awards and honors. Rather, it should be said that he tried to "feed the hungry, clothe the naked, be right on the Vietnam War and love and serve humanity."[21]

Dr. Martin Luther King, Jr. was an American clergyman who became America's civil rights champion. A leader of the Civil Rights Movement and a Nobel laureate, he was an honored member of our coalition we would sorely miss.

Sixty-three days after King's assassination, Senator Robert F. Kennedy was killed at the Ambassador Hotel in Los Angeles after winning the California presidential primary. Kennedy had announced the night he was murdered that the country was ready to end its fractious divisions. His body lay in repose at St. Patrick's Cathedral in New York for two days but his impact on the country was especially apparent when his body was transported by a slow-moving train from New York to Washington, D.C. The television public watched thousands of tearful, sullen mourners lining the tracks over hundreds of miles as the nation paid its final respects.

In a year of public assassinations and street violence in hundreds of cities, the Johnson administration had no desire to see riots outside its national convention. Ramsey Clark, Attorney General for the Johnson administration, dispatched Roger Wilkins, one of his top aides, to meet with me in our South Dearborn office building. Wilkins was an Assistant Attorney General and one of the highest-ranking blacks ever to serve in the executive branch up to that time. We spent hours getting acquainted, both of us cautious and each of us full of questions. I wanted to know whether the Johnson administration held a different position than Mayor Daley on our right to protest and petition the government. Wilkins wanted to know whether I was committed along with our large coalition to nonviolence in Chicago. It took time, but as we talked and listened, we came to trust each other. In fact, we liked each other. Wilkins later stated that I "was a person who was telling me the truth" and I felt the same about him. When he subsequently met with Mayor Daley and his mention of "Rennie Davis" turned the Mayor's neck crimson red followed by a

---

21 Wikipedia. "Assassination of Martin Luther King, Jr." Wikipedia describes the eulogy from Dr. King at his own funeral. https://en.wikipedia.org/wiki/Assassination_of_Martin_Luther_King,_Jr.

twenty-five-minute impassioned monologue from the Mayor, he knew without a doubt that there would be no permits granted in Chicago that summer. The Mayor made it perfectly clear that the Justice Department's position that Chicago should grant permits for legal and peaceful demonstrations would not be entertained in the Windy City that summer. That meant I had to prepare for an event whose outcome could not be predicted.

SEE YOU
IN
CHICAGO
AUG. '68

Permit negotiations with the city continued in earnest but started to feel like a bizarre plot drawn up for a Hollywood suspense movie. Following each "negotiating" session in the Mayor's office, I would give my account of what happened to the assembled press. Every U.S. television network carried the story as the issue of permits became an American daily obsession. While the mention of my name seemed to turn Mayor Daley's neck crimson red, the official who represented the Mayor was surprisingly calm, cool and collected. He was also in complete alignment with his name—David Stahl—stalling us every step of the way. At first, I thought his last name was a coincidence until I entered a federal court room to petition Chicago courts for permits. The U.S. District Court judge who instantly ruled for the city upon hearing my case was Daley's former law partner and his name was William Lynch—seriously.

One day at my downtown office, the drama got even stranger. Two men in plain clothes flashed their badges at me and said they were undercover agents from the Chicago Police Department. They let me know they would follow me...basically forever. I thought someone had to be making this up until police tails became another part of my bizarre Chicago experience.

Years later, a Cook County grand jury concluded that members of the Chicago Police Department's security section had spied on peace groups "for political reasons," and seventy-one witnesses and 5,000 pages of subpoenaed documents convinced the jurors to condemn the Police Department's intelligence gathering abuses—but that finding came too late for me.

The first day I met my first police tails, they let me know with a rather menacing tone that it would be hazardous to my health to "shake them". That was how it began and continued for years. When the Chicago protest was over, undercover agents continued to park outside my apartment at night, waiting for me to wake up. They followed me to meetings. They followed me to airports where other agents met me as I deplaned. Only when I entered a country they couldn't access—like

Yippie Candidate for President

David Fenton Photo

Vietnam—did I have a few weeks of freedom from my "red squad" tails. Otherwise, surveillance was part of my routine. I decided not to let it bother me and got rather skilled at shaking my tails too. But my greatest accomplishment was when one of them became a friend—which happened as well.

I appreciated that an urban police force has a difficult job, especially when a city seems poised on the precipice of mayhem. Chicago's police force had 11,900 men and women who were in a preparation mode for months before the convention. In the days leading up to the August world spectacle, they went to twelve-hour shifts and kept adding more personnel just to be "ready." Supported by 7,500 Army troops, 7,500 Illinois National Guardsmen, and 1,000 Secret Service agents, additional security personnel and FBI agents were brought in to guard the convention delegates. Fire marshals were on hand as well, and police marksmen with high powered rifles were at the ready. *Life Magazine* ran an article stating the U.S. Navy had stationed a secret submarine in Lake Michigan to spy on protest leaders.

Abbie Hoffman and Jerry Rubin were among those protest leaders and they had police tails too. As the spokesmen for a youth group called the Youth International Party (Yippies), they were known for their humor and ridicule when mocking Mayor Daley. Abbie especially had a rare talent when it came to poking the public's funny bone at the Mayor's expense. Many times, I watched him get an entire press corps laughing out loud.

The Yippies' purpose in Chicago was to stage a "real circus" to satirize the "political circus" going on at the Amphitheatre.

One day, Jerry and Abbie proudly announced their presidential candidate called "Pigasus"—a large white pig they paraded down the streets of Chicago running for the highest office in the land. They also claimed the city's drinking water would be treated with the hallucinogenic drug, LSD. Reporters got the joke, but a horrified Mayor Daly dispatched twenty-four-hour police guards to every pumping and filtration station in the city.

All the so-called "leaders" of the Chicago protest were tailed by undercover police. Pretending to be protesters, undercover squads infiltrated every movement organization coming to Chicago. One agent was so proud of his stealthy skills infiltrating the Yippies, he described a meeting making plans for a Yippie

Mother's Day march. The undercover agent told his story to a reporter. The Yippies wanted to present apple pies to the 18th district police station and the police agent attended a planning meeting he described to a reporter.

"[They] all sat around a flashing light, talking, drinking, and blowing pot. No one even questioned me when I wandered in."[22] According to the reporter's account, Peter Keer thought the best way to get the names of everyone attending the Yippie planning meeting was to have the police raid the apartment. He directed uniformed patrolmen to bang on the door with a search warrant. Thirteen men were arrested for disorderly conduct and seven women were booked for being inmates of a disorderly house. By mid-August, Lincoln Park was overrun with these undercover "professionals." Yippies would tease them with questions like, "Don't you think I'm as dangerous as Abbie Hoffman?" They had fun with each other too, exclaiming with a pretend chagrin that "your cops are better looking than my cops!"

Peter Keer described the details of his surveillance of Abe Peck and Abbie Hoffman as they ordered breakfast one morning. He said, "I took a seat near the door, avoiding eye contact by staring into the menu. Abbie was sitting at the counter and turned around and gave me the finger. When Abe and Abbie left the diner to head for the park, I followed. We were not too worried about losing them in the park," he said. "When Peck and Hoffman reached Lake Shore Drive, however, the two broke into a trot. Before we knew it, they ran across eight lanes of traffic and jumped into a van waiting in the emergency outlet across the road. Then away they went, northbound on the drive, waving at us."[23]

To lose my police tails, I used stealthy tricks too and loved them when they worked—which was most every time.

As we got closer to the convention, I knew it was Plan B for us. That meant setting up in Lincoln Park far from the convention hall. Our coalition decided to follow an established Chicago tradition, however. Boy Scouts had been permitted to stay overnight in Lincoln Park, and the city had supported other

---

22 *Reader*. "Confessions of a Red Squad Spy: A former Police Department intelligence agent recalls the dirty tricks of 1968." Reported by Lynn Emmerman. August 25, 1975.
23 Ibid.

groups staying overnight in the park as well. Since our antiwar coalition had insufficient funds to house thousands of people in hotels, the Chicago Boy Scout tradition seemed a good strategy. Demonstrators coming to the city who couldn't afford hotel rooms could stay in the park like the Boy Scouts.

Our permit "negotiations" had two objectives: 1) staying overnight in Lincoln Park, and 2) marching to the Amphitheatre on the night of the presidential nomination. The march to the Amphitheatre was ten miles from Lincoln Park and was planned for August 28, the night of the nomination. Unfortunately, we received no permits for Lincoln Park or for the march to the Amphitheatre but at the last moment, we were granted a permit to hold an afternoon rally in downtown Grant Park, close to where the delegates stayed in hotels. I knew people who lived in Chicago would join our protest if we had a permit so I said yes to the city's last minute offer.

Preparing for Chicago meant preparing for unknown contingencies. Since we did not know exactly what would happen, I wanted a marshal organization that was flexible and could communicate under pressure with the entire demonstration in fast moving conditions. Our team organized a large medical support network and an even larger contingent of marshals—volunteers who were mostly in their twenties who could support communication with demonstrators in the event of volatile street activities.

One day, I asked our marshals to congregate in Lincoln Park for a training exercise and hundreds of activists linked arms and moved in the form of a snake dance, practicing a Japanese martial arts maneuver. The press went completely a-twitter, watching us shout "Wasshoi!" While we had no intention to use this maneuver during the demonstrations, our marshals' ability for rapid response was truly outstanding, and shocked the police every time we did anything together.

Lincoln Park was our initial staging ground for a demonstration the whole world would witness. A beautiful area north of downtown Chicago, the park was 3.189 square miles running along the Chicago lakefront from Ohio Street Beach in the Streeterville neighborhood northward to Ardmore Avenue in Edgewater. The park included the Lincoln Park Zoo, Theatre on the Lake, and Lincoln Park Conservatory. This was where the world mayhem event would begin. Present that first night were the famous poets Allen Ginsberg and William Burroughs, along with French poet Jean Genet. I appreciated Allen Ginsberg's "OM" chanting in the park because it seemed to calm everyone down.

I wanted demonstrators to be safe, but knew we had to prepare for fluid crowd movements in the event we were driven into Chicago neighborhoods by force. As the first evening of the convention opened and the delegates were gaveled to order, Mayor Daley formally opened the convention by making his own mission in Chicago crystal clear: "As long as I am mayor of this city, there's going to be law and order in Chicago."

On the first morning of the convention demonstration, Tom Hayden was abruptly arrested and I didn't know why. I was concerned. Our marshals organized a march to the police station to 'free Tom.' After a large gathering spontaneously assembled, we walked from Lincoln Park toward the police headquarters at 11th and State, using sidewalks and the street, as necessary. As we got closer to the police station, the tension became palpable. I was in the front of the march and could see police had surrounded us. It felt like the smallest incident could ignite beatings or even gunfire. To my relief, we were able to leave the area unharmed, and Tom was discharged and released later that day.

As we returned to Lincoln Park, thousands of young people were enjoying the musicians who had come to perform at our festival of life. The park hours were 6:00 a.m. to 11:00 p.m. As we approached the witching hour, Chicago policemen began gathering in large numbers at the park's edge. I knew they would bring chaos to the park if they cleared the area, but never imagined the mayhem that was about to commence. At 11:00 pm sharp, orders were given to clear the area and tear gas filled the grounds with great billowy, eerie clouds that looked like film footage from a war zone. Batons swung like baseball bats bashing heads in their wake. We had our medics, and cloths to filter the effects of the burning gas, but when the police charged the park, our traditional nonviolent resistance strategy—sit down and peacefully be carried off to jail—was not in the cards. Our plan was to stay nonviolent, but clear of the clubbing police, if possible. While most demonstrators were able to move out of the park safely into surrounding neighborhoods, hundreds of people were beaten that first night, including reporters from network television stations and Chicago residents who were brazenly pulled off their home porches by police. Beating the press, Chicago residents and hundreds of demonstrators turned the first night into a world media event. This was just the beginning too. Over the course of the week, seventeen reporters were attacked by Chicago police. Just like Donald Trump, the police managed to turn the American press assembled in Chicago into their "enemy."

Bobby Seale

The second day of the Convention, 200 members of the American Friends Service Committee marched to the Amphitheatre from a North Side church. As more people joined in, the numbers grew to about 1,000. They were stopped half a mile from the Amphitheatre, where they camped out until 10 a.m. the next day. Their march was the closest any of us got to the convention hall that week.

In the early evening of the second day, Black Panther Party Chairman Bobby Seale arrived in Chicago and spoke in Lincoln Park. I had invited Eldridge Cleaver to speak, but at the last minute, he couldn't come and asked Bobby to take his place. I had never met Bobby and wouldn't until a year later in a courtroom where we were accused of planning a conspiracy together that caused the Chicago riots. Bobby made two speeches in Chicago, and for his "crime" of speech, he would face ten years in federal prison. He wrote *Seize the Time*, a book about his experience that is relevant again today.

During the second night in Lincoln Park, several hundred clergy and lay church people brought a twelve-foot cross into the park and vowed to remain past the 11 p.m. curfew. I explained to them that being carried off to jail in a nonviolent protest would not be possible in this openly hostile police environment. I suggested that when the police charged, they should pull out and retreat. But they decided to stay. It took courage to sit with their cross and they were badly beaten too.

Tuesday night in Lincoln Park was especially brutal. Hundreds of police massed at the eastern end and moved westward behind a thick cloud of tear gas shot from gas guns and supplemented by a gas truck. With gas masks on, the police cleared the area with their swinging batons largely invisible to us inside that blizzard of harsh, thick tear gas. I wanted to leave the park and go downtown and our marshals responded by talking with thousands of demonstrators individually about going where the delegates had their hotel rooms. We re-assembled on Michigan Avenue in front of the Conrad Hilton so the delegates would see us when they returned from the convention.

My hope for today's movement is that the importance of marshals when organizing fluid, dynamic events will be thoroughly embraced. Our marshals were exceptional that night in Chicago, spreading the word to thousands of people who were fleeing the chaos that everyone should go downtown—which everyone did.

Turning an outdoor garbage can upside down for a speaker's platform, we emerged from our Lincoln Park shadows to speak openly to the country. That night, our speakers were elegant and their passion soared. At one point, everyone started to chant, "The whole world is watching! The whole world is watching!" not fully realizing that hundreds of millions of people were literally watching us around the world. The police decided to back away from our garbage can stage and let us be. They were quickly replaced by the Illinois National Guard. As the guard moved in, I appreciated the fact that these replacement troops had no problem allowing us to exercise our right to free speech and say in public why we had come to Chicago in the first place.

The third day of the convention was the presidential nomination—the only day our coalition had been granted a permit for an afternoon demonstration in Grant Park. A 319-acre site, Grant Park had performance venues inside beautiful, mature gardens.

Lake Michigan bordered the park's east side, and Chicago's business district was to the west. Even with six hundred policemen surrounding us and National Guardsmen stationed on the roof of the nearby Field Museum, our rally was festive, passionate and mostly fear-free.

After two violent days in Chicago, I was amazed by the turnout of mothers with children in strollers. People in their twenties were our largest constituency by far but our permit was meant to assure safety for an assembly of people of any age. That was our belief until a teenager went to the flagpole at 3:30 p.m. and lowered the American flag to half-mast. According to his testimony in the Chicago Eight trial after the convention, that half-mast flag was a symbol of international distress. The police who gathered on the western side of our legal public venue didn't see it that way. With orders from Deputy Police Superintendent James Rochford to arrest the teenager, they charged our gathering, capturing and beating the teenager as they carried him through screaming protesters and flying objects. I called on our marshals, and in a few short moments, an impressive line of young men and women with locked arms were facing the police with a human perimeter that separated our rally from the uniformed police. With one swift motion, everyone calmed down. The police, however, were taken aback—okay, freaked out—by the precision of our marshals.

I got on a bullhorn in front of the marshals and addressed the police, saying, "We have a permit. This is a legal demonstration, and we need you to pull back so we can continue our legal rally." My words were like kerosene on a fire and ignited the police to charge again. I could hear some of them yelling, "Kill Davis! Kill Davis!" above the screams and shouts behind me as they descended on the gathering. My super-skilled martial arts bodyguard was incapacitated with a broken leg, and I was struck down, too. A swinging baton landed on the top of my head, knocking me down, dazed but still conscious. With my survivor instinct heightened, I propelled myself forward, crawling with both arms flailing, as police batons repeatedly rained down on my back and legs. For a moment, the thought crossed my mind that "I'm not getting out of here." Fortunately, my bright savior that day was a chain-link fence. Clawing myself forward on the ground, I was able to slide under the fence, giving myself a few precious seconds to stand up and disappear into the crowd. Helping hands assisted me to the far side of our rally site where I passed out. When I regained awareness, my first sensation was feeling relief that my glasses had not been broken. Then I heard Tom Hayden from the stage giving an account of what had just happened to me. When he learned I was bleeding on the ground, he told demonstrators that the police were not going to let us out of the park for a march to the Amphitheatre. Tom said everyone should leave in small groups and not be trapped by the police in a large march. He urged everyone to re-assemble in front of the downtown hotels where the nation and the delegates could see us. One of my best friends and a leader of our coalition, Dave Dellinger, disagreed with Tom. He wanted people to march to the Amphitheatre. When the effort to march was blocked by police, he worried later that he might have "led the group into a trap". While our leadership had its moment of tactical disagreement, everyone went back to the Hilton in downtown Chicago and came together as the evening of the nomination shifted the national story from inside the convention to the streets of Chicago.

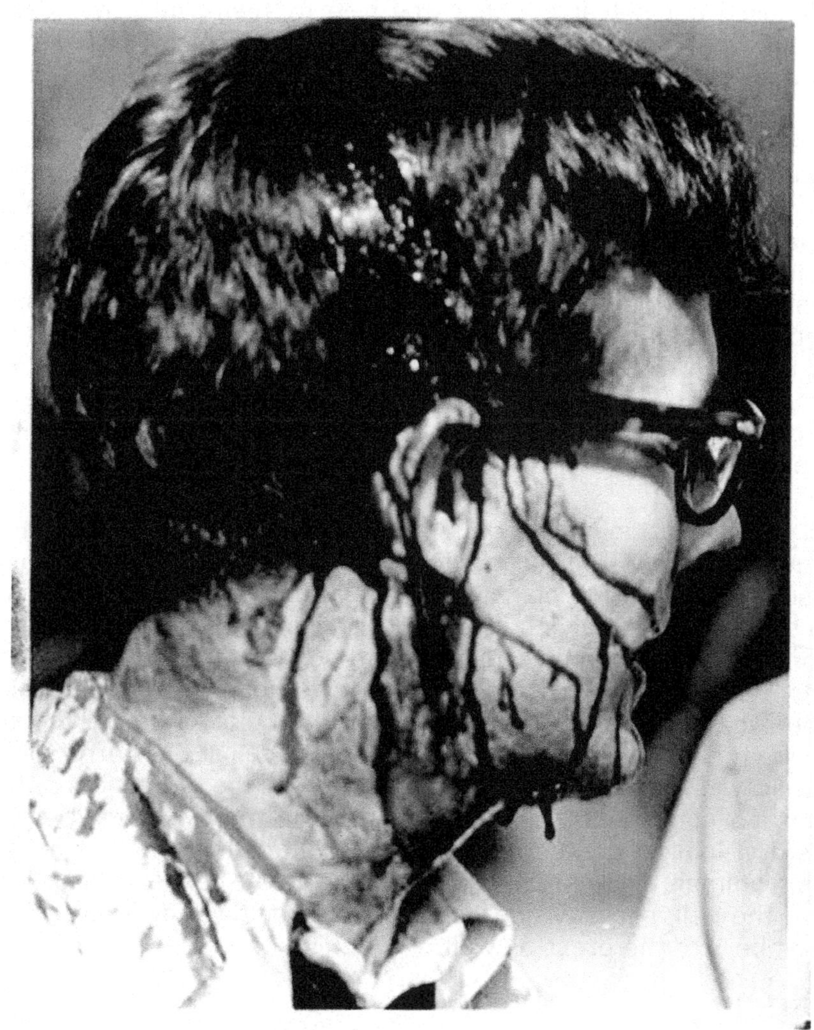

Grant Park Beating

I was hurried out of the park by our medics and taken to a county hospital for thirteen stitches in my head. The police nightstick left a skull indentation I can feel today. Because I was clubbed by police but not arrested, I was free to speak with the press about what had happened. That was a problem for the police who seemed desperate to quiet me by arresting me.

The hospital medical staff were city employees who had been watching us on television. When the police arrived at the hospital to conduct a room-by-room search to arrest me, my imaginary screenplay writer came up with another whopper. I could hardly believe that a few courageous members of the hospital medical team literally risked their careers to hide me, pushing my mobile bed from room to room, evading the police search, until they came to an exit and I was able to escape. I was never arrested in Chicago, but had to retreat to the safe house of a friend where I watched the chaotic presidential nomination on television with the rest of a stunned world audience.

The organization founded by Martin Luther King, Jr. brought a mule wagon to Chicago to symbolize America's poor and disenfranchised. The plan was to bring their "Poor People's March" to the delegates staying at the Conrad Hilton on the night of the nomination. As a world audience watched Chicago police beating and clubbing demonstrators outside the hotels, the mule train entered the fray and was brutally assaulted too. As the delegates inside the convention began to speak out against the horrors the public was watching on television outside the convention, the Chicago convention transformed into the most violent in U.S. history—police beating protesters, bystanders and the mule train animals alike. As the violence outside the convention spilled into the hall, security guards roughed up antiwar delegates and members of the press as well.

Grant Park Interview

It had been an unimaginable week for the convention delegates. They arrived in a city under siege to encounter a telephone strike, bus strike, and taxi strike at the same time. The two opposing sides—antiwar delegates and law and order delegates—erupted into open conflicts inside the Democratic Party while the whole world was watching. A drama beyond any Hollywood imagination, it wasn't between protesters and police anymore. Delegates to the convention were divided and the nation was polarized as well.

Mayor Daley set the tone for the convention week by greeting the delegates with his pronouncement, "We have no flag burners in this Democratic Convention." Daley's ushers took that to mean that they had the Mayor's permission to hassle, push, and shove antiwar delegates for wearing McCarthy or McGovern pins on their lapels.

The leading candidate for President—Vice President Hubert Humphrey—had been a political progressive most of his career, but was dependent on Lyndon Johnson in seeking the highest office in the land. When Humphrey tried to get a plank in the platform that could give some support to the large antiwar constituency inside the Democratic Party, he called Johnson to read the proposed language but Johnson instantly struck it down. Throughout the convention week, America's television audience watched the intense scuffling and yelling among the delegates. As the tension reached the boiling point, Mayor Daley's decision to beat and club demonstrators in broad daylight outside the convention hall became a turning point for the American public.

When an antiwar plank was defeated by a majority of convention delegates, antiwar delegates marched through the aisles singing "We Shall Overcome." Mayor Daley responded by giving the signal to drown out the protest song with "Strike Up the Band." As the conflict in the streets spilled into the convention, CBS newsmen Mike Wallace and Dan Rather were punched in the face by security guards on camera. While trying to interview a Georgia delegate, Dan Rather was grabbed by Daley's guards and roughed up. He was later heard on national television telling the guards, "Don't push me. Take your hands off unless you plan to arrest me." When the guards let go, he told his colleague Walter Cronkite on air, "Walter...we tried to talk to this man and we got violently pushed out of the way. This is the kind of thing that has been going on outside the hall—but this is the first time we've had it happen inside the hall. I'm sorry to be out of breath, but somebody belted me in the stomach." Walter Cronkite, America's most distinguished news anchor in history, could only say to a national audience, "I think we've got a bunch of thugs here, if I may be permitted to say so."[24]

In his speech nominating George McGovern for president, Connecticut Senator Abraham Ribicoff criticized the "Gestapo tactics on the streets of Chicago" on national television. As the cameras zoomed in on an enraged, red-faced Daley, the mayor was seen shouting back at the rostrum. Ted Sorenson, a prominent advisor to President Kennedy, took the podium and said, "We are not outside the Democratic Party. We agree with every Democratic primary—stop the war."

When it came to covering the beatings in the streets, however, the media was conflicted. Television executives had to decide whether their television coverage should stay focused on the proceedings of a national nominating convention or let the television audience see the police beatings of demonstrators outside. The media eventually cut away from the divided convention to watch the story outside—police clubbing demonstrators, newsmen, medics and the Mule Train—in what was later called a police riot by a national investigation into what happened in Chicago.

That was the real story of this convention and the whole world was watching the horror of a police riot on television. Many American voters who had traditionally supported their government in matters of war were simply fed up and turned their thumbs down on the Vietnam War because of the Chicago convention mayhem.

Hubert Humphrey waited for the vote tally in his Conrad Hilton room on the twenty-fifth floor. When he opened his hotel window to see what was happening on the streets below, staff members in his room said the tear gas could be smelled through his open window. When his nomination was secured and a lifetime ambition was realized, there was no celebration in the wreckage of the evening. Humphrey's room felt like a wake, and his family and close associates were utterly depressed. Convention delegates against the war walked out of the hall to join a candlelight vigil. The nation watched in disbelief as Chicago acquired a unique place in history. Public fury over a war in a distant jungle had torn

24 *CBS Evening News*. August 27, 1968.

the Democratic Party asunder. The battle of Michigan Avenue in front of the Conrad Hilton sparked a change in the mood of the country.

While middle-aged adults who were against the war felt they had to stay home rather than risk violence in Chicago, people in their twenties came to the city anyway. As the public watched live coverage of the brutal assault of America's sons and daughters by Chicago police, the public took back their blank check for the government's war policies in Vietnam.

The day following the nomination, I returned to our downtown makeshift venue in front of the Hilton ready to participate again. Looking like a Civil War poster, my head was wrapped in a blood-stained bandage as I tried to see out of the wrappings. I stood on top of our upside-down garbage can and said what everyone around me already knew. "We are the sons and daughters of a nation living in a deeply divided time. The Vietnam War is coming home. For the sake of our GIs, our country, and every human being living in Indochina, we know what the United States must do. Bring our GIs home. This war must end here and now."

The arrest count for the convention week tallied 668. Hospitals reported treating 111 demonstrators, although most of our injured demonstrators didn't go to the hospital. Our medical volunteers estimated they treated over 1,000 demonstrators. The police department reported 192 officers were injured with 49 requiring hospital treatment. That same week, 308 Americans were killed in Vietnam and another 1,144 were injured.

The events in Chicago ignited a new wave of public opinion against the war but it hardly mattered. Since Richard Nixon was the only option offered by America's two-party system and the Democratic Party was in ruin after Chicago, Nixon was elected president. The Democratic Party that conducted the war was humiliated so the Republicans won. Since no Republican administration was going to go down in history for losing a war, the new administration expanded the war by invading Cambodia.

The Sixties Movement learned not to be tied to any single election cycle. Some elections can make a difference but Movements to change the world change societies.

After the Chicago convention, the public wanted to know who caused the Chicago riots. Milton Eisenhower, who chaired the National Commission on the Causes and Prevention of Violence, announced his commission would investigate and report its findings to President Lyndon Johnson. A Chicago lawyer, Daniel Walker, headed a team of over 200 investigators who interviewed more than 1,400 witnesses and studied FBI reports and film footage of the confrontations. *The Walker Report*, released on December 1, 1968, labeled the convention violence a "police riot" and recommended prosecution of the police who used indiscriminate violence. While the report acknowledged many Chicago police behaved professionally, the failure to prosecute the individuals who misbehaved would only further damage public confidence, Walker said. While the report described the language used by some demonstrators and noted there was provocation of the police, it blamed the violence on the city's refusal to grant permits. When *The Walker Report* was published, it shot straight to the top of *The New York Times* bestseller list and was one of the better summaries of my own purpose in Chicago—to seek permits for a large-scale nonviolent demonstration against the war in Vietnam. Our coalition had done it before, and would do it again. Nearly 500,000 people marched non-violently through Washington, D.C. the year following our protest in Chicago. No one was clubbed and beaten in Washington a year later either.

The Chicago police said they had been the targets of epithets and rocks hurled at them by demonstrators and *The Walker Report* confirmed that did occur. It also concluded that those events were provoked by police actions. When the police were put on edge by media reports of city disruption, the official response was indiscriminate police violence, particularly at night. *The Walker Report* said that violence was often inflicted upon persons "who had broken no law, disobeyed no order and made no threat, including peaceful demonstrators, onlookers, newsmen and large numbers of residents simply passing through or living in areas where confrontations were occurring." It said that newsmen and photographers were especially singled out for assault and their equipment deliberately damaged. Fundamental police training was ignored and police officers refused (or were unable) to control their men. In answering the question, who caused the riots in Chicago, *The Walker Report* concluded that police violence was the fundamental fact of the convention week.[25]

On March 20, 1969, a Chicago grand jury rejected the findings of *The Walker Report*.

Instead of the Mayor and hundreds of baton-swinging police being indicted, eight civilians and eight policemen were indicted. All the police were found not guilty. The eight civilians, however, were charged under provisions of the 1968 Civil Rights act that made it a federal crime to cross state lines with the intention to incite a "riot." This was new legislation that targeted what a person said or wrote when determining their intention. I was one of the Chicago Eight defendants, and knew immediately that what had just happened in the streets of Chicago would now be prosecuted in a federal courtroom. For me, being indicted wasn't horrible news. In fact, it made me smile.

From a federal courtroom in Chicago, our movement would now prosecute the government's war in Vietnam before a world audience.

25 Walker, Daniel. *Rights in Conflict: Convention Week in Chicago*, August 25-29, 1968: A Report. New York: E.P. Dutton, 1968.

Chapter 5

THE CHICAGO SEVEN

Trial of the Century

The year 1969 harbored some of the dark memories of 1637. That was the year Anne Hutchinson was cast out of the Massachusetts Bay Colony for her religious and ideological differences with the Puritan government to become one of the early historical markers of America's repressive tradition. The rise of Donald J. Trump has roots in that dark past as well. From Salem witch hunts to mob lynchings in the South, a democratic country that inspired a better world has had its dark side too. America's chronicle of slavery, bigotry, witch hunts, tar and feather episodes, cross burnings, and blacklist name calling is part of our own history.

In 1850, Nathaniel Hawthorne described this dark tradition using the image of a Scarlet Letter—in a novel bearing the same name. Hester Prynne was forced to wear a Scarlet Letter as a mark of public humiliation for committing adultery and having a child out of wedlock. Scarlet Letters have happened before and are still the favorite gift to give by a segment of our country.

In the 1950s, America's dark side was called "blacklisting." A Cold War climate was fueling a witch-hunt culture inside American politics. People refusing to testify before a Congressional committee investigating "communism" could have their families torn asunder and their careers vilified and ruined. Public humiliation was the objective of these Congressional witch hunts and the rule of law was routinely trampled by whipping up the hysteria of the Republican Party mob to embolden their elected representatives to rekindle and enflame the country's repressive tradition.

The issuance of a Congressional subpoena by the House Un-American Activities Committee had the same motivation as the issuance of a Scarlet Letter.

In the 1950s, two close friends could suddenly collide like a shipwreck as a family's reputation vanished beneath the waves. Creative screenplays and films were shelved, out of fear of their political consequences. Movies like *Salt of the Earth* were banned. Studio films championing the social outcast or underdog became favorite political targets. The American educational system was a magnet for the country's anticommunist fury too. Some people getting their Scarlet Letter felt so humiliated they took their own lives. When an "ex-communist" desperately wanted his job back after getting a Scarlet Letter from the House Un-American Activities Committee, he had to repent by naming his "sympathizers." The American political climate moved so far to the right that ostracizing "totalitarian liberals" became an accepted practice in the United States Congress.

Border walls and demonizing entire religions have their roots in the Scarlet Letter tradition of America's troubled past.

That's why this Sixties story is relevant again. What we did to HUAC when we got our Scarlet Letters could be helpful to today's movement setting out to change the world.

Joseph McCarthy was a Wisconsin Republican and a crusader for the 1950s version of the Salem Witch Trials. At the 1952 Republican Chicago Convention, he stirred the national delegates into a standing ovation with his words of thunder:

> My good friends, I say one Communist in a defense plant is one Communist too many. One Communist on the faculty of one university is one Communist too many. One Communist among the American advisers at Yalta is one Communist too many. And even if there were only one Communist in the State Department, that would still be one Communist too many.

At the eye of the 1950s political storm, the House Un-American Activities Committee (HUAC) fueled the hate and fury like no one else. Created to investigate "the extent, character and objects of Un-American propaganda activities," its "investigations" targeted democratic dissent and progressive politics in any form whatsoever. Like today, when the 1950s Republican Party gained control of both houses of Congress in 1954 and dirty politics became fair game for advancing the fear and divide agenda of that era, Trump-style fear tactics won elections up and down the ballot. With repression and hate gaining popular momentum, the Supreme Court weighed in too. The highest court in the land ruled that a "teacher shapes the attitude of young minds towards the society in which they live" and school authorities have the right and the duty to screen the officials, teachers, and employees as to their fitness to maintain the integrity of the schools as a part of ordered society—that "cannot be doubted."[26]

By the time I was named to stand among the heroes who had been called to testify before HUAC, the Committee's influence was waning. Because of the fury of our movement and the support of progressive Democrats who refused to compromise on America's core values, McCarthyism was losing its sting. Over time, HUAC came under public attack for its bully tactics by Congress itself. Even former President Harry Truman denounced the Committee as the most "un-American thing in the country today."

While the mindset of hate is part of America's dark tradition, another part has been our times of waking up. Waking up is also part of our history. When a new generation wakes up, fear and divide loses its grip. The 1950s did not have a movement to push back on the dark side, but the 1960s did—and that made all the difference. When I was subpoenaed by HUAC with others from the Chicago 7, we were dealt a hand of cards that granted us a special honor and privilege—pulling the plug on HUAC's life support system, and shutting it down once and for all.

In 1969, as I was heading to a Chicago federal courtroom, I was ordered to stop at the Capitol in Washington, D.C. A Scarlet Letter was waiting from the infamous Congressional committee. While Congressional scarlet Letters had happened many times before, this time was different. A movement existed. Having a movement changed everything. The Sixties movement was the official and powerful American push back to Scarlet Letters, witch hunts, bigotry and racism of every variety. With HUAC beginning to lose its wallop, 1969 seemed a good year to yank the repressive dark side into the light—and that's exactly what happened.

---

26 U.S. Supreme Court, Adler v. Board of Education of City of New York, 342 U.S. 485, Decided March 3, 1952.

Since Scarlet Letters are coming back today, we need a new generation to put an end to this sad, dark practice. As the banner of hate resurfaces in the present time, today's movement changes everything.

A movement pushes the dark side with its false news and relentless bigotry to reflect on itself. When a person demonizes a neighbor for their race, religion, or station in life, they have the argument when a movement is sweeping the land. A movement turns on the spot light and illuminates our darkest alleys. It is the great antigen to Scarlet Letters.

When we were subpoenaed to pick up our Scarlet Letters, here's what we did.

Reason and common sense are a powerful push back to fear and divide when you have tens of millions of people standing up for humanity but nothing works better than a barrel of humor to dampen the fire of a bigoted bullying Congressional committee. For Jerry Rubin, Abbie Hoffman, Tom Hayden, Dave Dellinger, and me, appearing before the notorious witch hunt Congressional HUAC, we had a giant advantage. We had movement. That gave us license to be playful and serve up recipes of humor and ridicule mixed with reason and common sense. It was a perfect recipe for ending the whole charade. Since we have tens of millions of people today mobilizing to resist the Trump effect, why not laugh and have fun inside the halls of Congress again?

The chairman of HUAC at the time we were called to testify was Representative Richard H. Ichord from Missouri. He tried his best to suppress our laughter and talking out loud by pounding his gavel and calling for order with his admonition: "Laughing, or any other emotional outburst, is out of order." Hell-bent and determined to have his witch hunt and push his Scarlet Letters in our direction, we were just as determined that laughter and reason would win the day—which it did. While previous witnesses greeted HUAC by defending their constitutional rights or making inspired emotional outbursts, they didn't have the support of a powerful movement. For us, we could share our vision of participatory democracy with the whole country while poking fun at the silliness and folly of the repressive Congressional mindset. Having a movement changes everything.

Jerry Rubin and David Dellinger

Proud Recipients of the Scarlet Letter
David Fenton Photo

Novelist Norman Mailer once said that to call on Jerry Rubin was "to call upon the most militant, unpredictable, creative—therefore dangerous—hippie-oriented leader available to the New Left." Jerry seemed to me the perfect lead-off witness for our Scarlet Letter push back. Jerry didn't dress in the traditional suit and tie and plead the Fifth Amendment. Instead, he put on an eighteenth century American Revolutionary War uniform and proudly announced he was a descendant of Thomas Jefferson and Tom Paine. "Nothing is more American than revolution," he said with an unabashed enthusiasm as he blew soap bubbles into the Congressional auditorium.[27] When Jerry visited HUAC again on December 4, he came as a bare-chested guerrilla dressed in Viet Cong pajamas with war paint, toting a toy M-16 rifle. When he got barred from entering the room, he showed up the next day dressed as Santa Claus and said to the press that he was dressed for a hearing that was a total circus.

When Abbie Hoffman was called to testify before the notorious Committee, he proudly held up his Scarlet Letter as though he had just won the Nobel Peace Prize. When asked the most dreaded, fearful question that HUAC possessed in its arsenal of fear: "Are you now, or have you ever been, a member of the Communist Party," he leaned into the microphone, and said with a completely straight face, "I refuse to answer the question on the grounds that it would tend to make me vomit."

Without the support of a movement, engaging the Committee like we did could earn you a ticket to jail. But with the support of a movement, however, sending us to prison for poking fun at this Congressional silliness would set off demonstrations throughout the United States. Everyone knew that too. To make this point crystal clear, the giant Congressional auditorium where we "testified" was filled to the brim with excited cheering supporters, most of them in their twenties. The national media turned out for the high drama too. I personally welcomed this opportunity to participate in a great public forum about the sickness of the Congressional witch-hunt. The attorney who represented me was dressed in a tight leather mini-skirt and she was hot. In other words, our spirit was festive and we were playful. We knew going in that by entering the hall with our irreverence for America's entire repressive tradition, we would confound and confuse this fading Congressional relic.

---

27 "Jerry Rubin." Wikipedia, the free encyclopedia. https://en.wikipedia.org/wiki/Jerry_Rubin

Jerry and Abbie were our comic, lead-off witnesses, and their irreverence was inspirational and priceless. Tom Hayden and I were our team's "straight men" who explained our mission to end the war with reason and logic. While I barely remember what I said, I found a transcript of what Tom said in *Thirty Years of Treason: Excerpts from Hearings before the House Committee on Un-American Activities, 1938-1968*. Here's what he said.

* * *

MR. CONLEY: Now, Mr. Hayden, were you the co-project director with Mr. [Rennie] Davis for the National Mobilization Committee's efforts in Chicago?

MR. HAYDEN: Yes, I was.

MR. CONLEY: By whom were you appointed?

MR. HAYDEN: By the Mobilization, which has a structure for making such appointments, consisting of an administrative committee and a steering committee and a set of officers

MR. CONLEY: Were you part of the steering committee or the officers or the—

MR. HAYDEN: No.

MR. CONLEY: In other words, you were appointed by this group. How many people are represented by this group?

MR. HAYDEN: The Mobilization has representatives from nearly a hundred organizations, most of whom are active around particular subjects like the organization of the demonstration.

MR. CONLEY: Well, did a hundred people meet to decide to appoint you?

MR. HAYDEN: I can't really recall. If you will allow me one minute to go talk to Rennie Davis, who has more of an organizational mind than I do, I am sure I could straighten it all out, but the Mobilization, through its normal process, appointed me in the spring of the year to be a project director with Rennie Davis, and I went to Chicago for that purpose.

* * *

MR. CONLEY: Mr. Hayden, is it your present aim to seek the destruction of the present American democratic system?

MR. HAYDEN: That is a joke.

MR. CONLEY: I am asking you, sir.

MR. HAYDEN: Well, I don't believe the present American democratic system exists. That is why we can't get together to straighten things out. You have destroyed the American democratic system by the existence of a committee of this kind.

MR. CONLEY: Well, let us use the word "system", then. Let us take the words "American" and "democratic" out of it and let us just call it the system. Is it your aim to destroy the present system?

MR. HAYDEN: What do you mean by "destroy"?

MR. CONLEY: To overturn it?

MR. HAYDEN: What do you mean by "overturn it"?

MR. CONLEY: To do away with it.

MR. HAYDEN: What do you mean by "do away with it"? By what means?

MR. CONLEY: I am asking you, sir.

MR. HAYDEN: No, you asked me whether it was my aim.

MR. CONLEY: I am asking you if that is your aim, sir.

MR. HAYDEN: The question is too ambiguous.

MR. CONLEY: Mr. Hayden, I have one final question for you. Ambrose Bierce, in his *Devil's Dictionary*, defines a conspirator as someone who finds it necessary to write down everything for his enemy to find. Mr. Hayden, you were clever enough not to be carrying any names or addresses on your person, or any slips of paper, at the time of the events in Chicago. However, in the purse of Miss Constance Brown was a complete list of names and addresses which were purportedly prepared by you. And I would ask you, sir, don't you think that the young people who follow you in these various movements should take a second look at you before they place their lives and their responsibilities in the hands [sic] of you?

MR. ICHORD: The witness will please be seated.

MR. HAYDEN: I thought that was the final question.

MR. ICHORD: The Chair directs the witness to be seated.

MR. WATSON: Mr. Chairman, may I make this point? I know there are advocates of free speech, and the witness is one of them, but I happen to be one who will not tolerate any such language as that. We have ladies in this room, and I shall not toleratie it, and if it is necessary for me to ask the police to arrest a man for such disorderly language as that, I shall do so. I am not going to tolerate language such as that in the presence of ladies.

MR. ASHBROOK: Mr. Hayden, sometimes I get the impression that you indicate what happened in Chicago was unfortunate, a travesty, and so forth. Other times, I get the indication you believe that Chicago was valuable, in that it demonstrated certain things, brought to the surface what you consider to be unfair treatment, some of the wrongs of the political processes. There is somewhat a dilemma here. I would like to have for the record whether you think now, looking back to the Chicago convention, what happened was good, bad, or helpful to your movement. You have talked kind of from both sides. I would like to know which is your honest point of view.

MR. HAYDEN: I have talked both sides, because we are going to win either way, Mr. Ashbrook. We would have won if it would have been safe and secure for two hundred thousand rank-and-file people, ordinary people, to come to Chicago and protest. That would have had a profoundly discrediting effect on the Democratic Party as it ratified the war in Vietnam and nominated Hubert Humphrey, and would have defeated the Democratic Party by the alienation of its grass-roots base. Since that was not allowed, because of the failure of the city to grant permits, since that was not allowed because there was too much jeopardy facing anybody with a family or job, and since they didn't come to Chicago, we won in a different way: by exposing the brute nature that underlies the supposedly democratic two-party system. I would have preferred to win the first way, but the second way was a tremendous victory of a kind for the young people in this country, people who watch on television and do not identify with the Nixon girls and David Eisenhower, but identify with the young people who are in the streets of Chicago, and watch very carefully... And that is a victory in the sense that committees like yourselves are now through. You exist only formally; but you have lost all authority. And when a group of people who have power lose their authority, then they have lost. You have lost, period. That is why I have been quiet. That is why these hearings aren't disrupted, that is why no one comes to these hearings to picket any more. The job has been done against HUAC, and the job has virtually been done against politicians.

MR. ICHORD: And you say you are eventually going to do the job against the whole United States?

MR. HAYDEN: Politicians like Dean Rusk, Lyndon Johnson, Richard Nixon, Hubert Humphrey, these people are in a sense already finished, because they can't exercise authority; they have no respect from wide sections of the American people. Richard Nixon does not even believe that Beatles albums should be played. He believes that drugs are the curse of American youth.

MR. ICHORD: Do you think that if you had performed the acts that you have performed and said such things that you have said in North Vietnam, in behalf of America, that you wouldn't be shot on the spot? Do you think you would be given the same amount of liberty, guarantees of First Amendment rights, which you have been given?

MR. HAYDEN: Mr. Ichord, I don't consider that I have that much freedom. Is it freedom to sit here, and under penalty of going to jail if I don't talk to you and express my opinions over and over in a committee chamber of this sort, knowing full well that the opinions are hot air, they have no effect on your ears, they will not change a thing? If that is freedom, that is a very inadequate definition of freedom.

MR. ICHORD: You have indeed a very strange philosophy, sir. You say that you don't care about electing a President. You don't care about a President at all. What kind of government do you want?

MR. HAYDEN: I want a democratic government...but I think the question at this point is a little bit redundant.[28]

* * *

The House Un-American Activities Committee was a legal inquisition that could subject any American citizen to punishment for their beliefs while denying subpoenaed witnesses their right to cross-examine anyone testifying against them. The Republican Party today would love to get away with this type of fear tactics again. Abandoning the rules of the courtroom allows "law and order" politicans to send witnesses to prison who are unwilling to cooperate. With Congress willing to disregard due process, it was our belief that the best approach to muzzling this attack dog on the Bill of Rights was to speak to our movement throughout the country. Since our movement was unwilling to be intimidated and would not compromise with Congressmen who smeared their opponents by trampling their rights, we stood up for America's core values. We returned to the American principle that a person is innocent until proven guilty. We declared the First Amendment would not be plucked from the American vision in our generation. Following our "testimony", the Congressional institution of Scarlet Letters literally imploded.

On February 18, 1969, a musty packet of Scarlet Letters was lowered into the grave and the House UnAmerican Activities Committee faded into oblivion.

Unfortunately, the myth of the dreaded Hydra—cutting off one head may cause two more to spring up—was still operating. When the head of the HUAC monster was severed in Washington, D.C., it sprang up again in a Chicago federal courtroom. Fortunately, the government's agenda in Chicago worked out about as well for them as the HUAC agenda in Washington, D.C.

---

28 Bentley, Eric, ed., *Thirty Years of Treason: Excerpts from Hearings before the House Committee on Un-American Activities*, 1938-1968. New York: Viking Press, 1971. p. 881-891.

Because Dr. Martin Luther King, Jr. had confronted the repressive tradition of slavery, racism, injustice, and unemployment, certain members of Congress wanted to blame him for the riots that followed his assassination. Embracing their Scarlet Letter tradition, some in Congress announced that their strategy would be to tar-and-feather the leaders.

In 1966, a Florida Congressional representative whose name was William Cramer introduced new legislation that made certain free speech a felony. Initially, it failed to pass, but following the King assassination, Representative William Cramer's bill became the law of the land. President Johnson and his Attorney General Ramsey Clark opposed this tar-and-feather strategy, but also wanted to secure passage of the 1968 Civil Rights Act. To compromise with the Republicans, President Johnson decided to accept the Cramer proposal. While the Department of Justice sent Congress a more "temperate" anti-riot bill, that bill was ignored. The Republicans wanted the harsher, anti-Martin Luther King legislation to stop the civil rights and antiwar leaders from speaking to the public.

The Civil Rights Act was an important legislative accomplishment. Making it a federal crime to intimidate blacks or civil rights activists working for voting enrollment, juries, employment, or the use of public accommodations, it created one of the most grievous assaults, on free speech in American history. That was the price Republicans extracted from the Democrats. The real motive behind the Cramer antiriot legislation was to silence our Movement by incarcerating our leaders.

The new legislation made it a crime to cross a state line and speak to an audience with the intent to incite a "riot." While a "riot" could be a small assembly of people standing on a street corner and their "crime' could be a misdemeanor, any words, written or spoken, could become evidence against a person charged with "inciting a "riot." With this new legislation, free speech that might stir up resistance to authority was deemed a felony.

To hear some in Congress tell it, "outside agitators" were the whole problem. There were Congressmen in the 1960s who actually believed that criminalizing the speech of Martin Luther King, Jr. was the "best solution" for dealing with the root causes of urban unrest. Many observers of the time started to call this new legislation the "outside agitator" law because it was squarely aimed at black leaders like Martin Luther King, Jr. and H. Rap Brown, who travelled from state to state through the South opposing America's racist practices.

The bright light of the Civil Rights law with its anti-riot dark side passed the Senate on March 11, 1968, but stalled in the more conservative House of Representatives due to the law's open housing provision. When riots broke out across the country in April, 1968 and U.S. troops ringed the Capitol building, Congress talked itself into a new round of Scarlet Letters as their best solution for dealing with the "outside agitators" causing the social problems of the nation.

The eight defendants in Chicago were indicted based on a twisted legal concept that made free speech a felony when you crossed a state line and madee statements against racism or foreign wars that stir people up. Of course, prominent constitutional lawyers came out of the woodwork to attend our trial and denounce the law as the worst assault on free speech in American history. Representative Emanuel Celler, Chairman of the House Judiciary Committee, described this legal nightmare with remarks printed in the Congressional Record. For starters, the anti-riot law, he said, violated the due process clause: The bill makes it a crime for an individual to cross a state line or mail a letter with an intent to encourage a riot. If a person later commits some overt act being co-conspirators not named as defendants herein, and with divers other persons, some known and others unknown to the Grand Jury, to commit offenses against the United States, that is:

INDICTMENT

The SEPTEMBER 1968 GRAND JURY charges:

1. Beginning on or about April 12, 1968, and continuing through on or about August 30, 1968, in the Northern District of Illinois, Eastern Division, and elsewhere,

DAVID T. DELLINGER,
RENNARD C. DAVIS,
THOMAS E. HAYDEN,
ABBOTT H. HOFFMAN,
JERRY C. RUBIN,
LEE WEINER,
JOHN R. FROINES and
BOBBY SEALE,

defendants herein, unlawfully, willfully and knowingly did combine, conspire, confederate and agree together and with

WOLFE B. LOWENTHAL
STEWART E. ALBERT,
SIDNEY M. PECK,
KATHIE BOUDIN,
SARA C. BROWN,
CORINA F. FALES,
BENJAMIN RADFORD,
BRADFORD FOX,
CRAIG SHIMABUKURO,
BO TAYLOR,
DAVID A. BAKER,
RICHARD BOSCIANO,
TERRY GROSS,
DONNA GRIPE,
BENJAMIN ORITZ,
JOSEPH TORNABENE
THOMAS W. NEUMANN,
and
RICHARD PALMER

a. to travel in interstate commerce and use the facilities of interstate commerce with the intent to incite, organize, promote, encourage, participate in, and carry on a riot and to commit acts of violence in furtherance of a riot, and to aid and abet persons in inciting, participating in, and carrying on a riot and committing acts of violence in furtherance of a riot, and during the course of such travel, and use, and thereafter, to perform overt acts for the purpose of inciting, organizing, promoting, encouraging, participating in, and carrying on a riot, and committing acts of violence in furtherance of a riot, and aiding and abetting persons in inciting, participating in, and carrying out a riot, and committing acts of violence in furtherance of a riot, in violation of Section 2101 of Title 18, United States Code;and

b. to teach and demonstrate to other persons the use, application, and making of incendiary devices, knowing, having reason to know, and intending that said incendiary devices would be unlawfully employed for use in and in furtherance of civil disorders which may obstruct, delay and adversely affect commerce and the movement of articles and commodities in commerce and the conduct and performance of federally protected functions, in violation of Section 231 (a) (I) of Title 18, United States Code; and,

c. to commit acts to obstruct, impede, and interfere with firemen and law enforcement officers lawfully engaged in the lawful performance of their official duties incident to and during the commission of civil disorders which obstruct, delay, and adversely affect commerce and the movement of articles and commodities in commerce and the conduct and performance of federally projected functions in violation of Section 231 (a) (3) of Title 18, United States Code.

2. It was a part of said conspiracy that from on or about April 12, 1968, through on or about August 24, 1968, the defendants DAVID T. DELLINGER, RENNARD C. DAVIS, THOMAS E. HAYDEN, ABBOTT H. HOFFMAN and JERRY C. RUBIN, and other coconspirators not named as defendants herein, would organize and attend various meetings, would publish and cause to be published articles, and would make and cause to be made long distance telephone calls for the purpose of encouraging persons to come to Chicago, Illinois, to participate in massive demonstrations during the period of on or about August 25, 1968, through on or about August 29, 1968.

> even though he no longer has that same intent, he will have violated the law even though his crossing of the state line occurred months or even years before. How a jury could possibly establish this intent unrelated to a contemporaneous act is impossible to fathom.[29]

On September 9, 1968, a Federal jury was empaneled to hear the government's evidence that eight Chicago "leaders" purportedly violated the "anti-riot law." If convicted, we faced a maximum imprisonment of five years. We were charged with violating the law and a conspiracy to violate the law. That conspiracy charge tacked on another five years for good measure. Even though former Attorney General, Ramsey Clark had discouraged the grand jury from issuing any indictments against demonstration leaders, and *The Walker Report* investigating what happened in Chicago found the Convention violence had been caused by police, Richard Nixon and his Attorney General enthusiastically supported these grand jury indictments.

That's how the "trial of the century" began. On March 20, 1969, I turned on my television to watch the news. I learned I had been indicated with seven others-Tom Hayden, Abbie Hoffman, Jerry Rubin, David Dellinger, Bobby Seale, Lee Weiner and John Froines by a grand jury for conspiring to cross state lines with the intent to incite a "riot" that "impeded policemen in their lawful duties."

All my friends called me up to celebrate the news. After the Democratic Convention had changed millions of people to oppose the Vietnam war, it was hard not to feel excitement for this new opportunity. The government was giving us a second chance to build public support for ending the war. My only regret was that no Latino, farm worker, or women activists were indicted too.

We were publicly known as the Chicago Eight until Bobby Seale was severed from the trial and the media changed our name to the Chicago Seven.

---

29 Congressional Record. 19373. Remarks of Representative Emanuel Celler in 1967.

Chicago 7 With Two Legal Champions

Leni Weinglass (far left)
William (Bill) Kunstler (far right)
David Fenton Photo

When people ask me today how the Chicago Eight were chosen, I can only speculate about the Justice Department's logic. They did pick key organizers of the convention protests—David Dellinger, Tom Hayden, Abbie Hoffman, Jerry Rubin, and me—but indicting Bobby Seale, who was a spokesman for the Black Panther Party and whose only role in Chicago consisted of making two talks in Lincoln Park, suggested they had other motives too. Why should Bobby face ten years in prison for two speeches? His indictment had nothing to do with what happened in Chicago. It had everything to do with what he represented to the government. The other two defendants, Lee Weiner and John Froines, were university professors. I speculated they were indicted to issue a warning to university teachers to stay clear of our movement. That was my guess for why they were chosen. What can be said for sure was that we were a mixed lot of defendants who did "conspire" to use the Chicago court proceedings to put the government on trial for the war in Vietnam.

We orchestrated a parade of celebrities, convention delegates, and demonstrators to keep the anti-war message in front of the public for the five-and-a-half-month proceedings. As defendants in a trial, we were not united on every issue either. We were eight people chosen by the government. Tom and I used reason and common sense as best we could when making our case but Abbie and Jerry went for humor and ridicule. David Dellinger was a war resister and pacifist in World War II—the oldest defendant who passionately opposed the Vietnam War. Bobby Seale was a founder of the Black Panther Party who advanced the "radical" proposition that black people had the right to defend themselves when they were physically attacked. John Froines and Lee Weiner were university professors who opposed the war and fully supported the Movement. People who knew us recognized we were an amalgam of lifestyles and politics but looking back, the sum of the parts was certainly greater than the whole.

Not everyone in the United States knew our names but everyone knew the Chicago 7.

On the trial's opening day, *The New York Times* wrote on its front page that this was "the most significant political trial in American history." Since the trial could not be televised and cameras were banned from the courtroom, the media relied on artist sketches to illustrate the daily drama for a world television audience.

The first motion before the judge came from our legal team, specifically Bobby Seale's lawyer, Charles Gerry. Gerry was facing an urgent gallbladder surgery and petitioned the court for a continuance so he could have his operation and return to the trial. While Chicago judges would typically grant a continuance for minor infractions like a parking violation, Judge Julius Hoffman denied our motion. In fact, he denied every motion of the defense throughout the five-and-a-half-month proceedings. By the end of the first day, people following the trial were wondering, who is Judge Julius Hoffman? With our first court appearance, our judge was the subject on everyone's mind.

President Eisenhower appointed Julius Jennings Hoffman to the U.S. District Court, and he had previously presided over high profile cases like Tony Accardo's tax evasion and Lenny Bruce's obscenity charges. Nothing, however, would compare to his role in the trial of the Chicago Eight.

Judge Hoffman entered the courtroom with a reputation for extraordinary courtroom abuse. One survey of Chicago lawyers concluded that nearly 80 percent of the professionals appearing before him had an unfavorable opinion. Without any pretense or modicum of impartiality, his scowls and hostility for us were on full public display. Years later, the executive committee of the U.S. District Court ordered that Hoffman not be assigned new cases due to his abusive and erratic behavior, but he somehow continued to preside over his court until the day he died.

Judge Hoffman had been randomly chosen for our trial. To me, having him for our judge was like winning the lottery.

With his blistering bias against us, he inflamed courtroom tensions simply by how he read the indictment against us, leaving no doubt that we were guilty as charged. He also repeatedly mispronounced our names, referring to our attorney Weinglass as "wild man" and calling Dave Dellinger "Dillinger" despite our lawyer's repeated corrections. A "fair and balanced" judge might have dampened public interest in a long tedious trial, but Judge Hoffman elevated the trial to the drama of great theatre on a global stage. He became the face of repression in charge of the trial of the century. While our message and mission constantly challenged the dark side of America's repression, Judge Hoffman made our case for us simply by entering the courtroom.

Although Judge Hoffman's reputation for exercising control over his courtroom was "mission impossible", given that we were the defendants, he tried valiantly. For example, when four of our pretrial attorneys withdrew from the case before the trial began, as we had always planned they would, Judge Hoffman held them in contempt and had two of them jailed. Only a nationwide protest of lawyers convinced him to back down and accept the defendants' choice for its defense team—William Kunstler and Leonard Weinglass.

When it came time to pick our jury, three hundred people were selected for the jury panel. Most were middle aged, middle class, and white. Our lawyers submitted fifty-four questions to the jurors, hoping to reduce the jury's cultural bias against us. We wanted to know whether a prospective juror knew the names of the country's rock 'n' roll stars. Who is Jimi Hendrix? Do you know the name Janis Joplin? We sneaked in a little rascal question for fun too—would you ever let your daughter marry a Yippie? Judge Hoffman rejected all of our fifty-four questions but one: Are you, or do you have any close friends or relatives who are, employed by law enforcement agencies? Among the many reasons for reversing our Chicago conviction, the Seventh Circuit Court of Appeal ranked the judge's refusal to permit our jury questions close to the top.

When the jury was finally seated, there were two white men and ten women, of whom eight were white. When the trial was over and the jurors could say what they really thought, one announced we should have been convicted for our appearance, language, and lifestyle. The foreman grumbled that we "wouldn't even stand up when the judge walked in." A third juror thought we "should have been shot down by the police." Author J. Anthony Lukas, who observed the trial for a book he was writing, described the jury as a "Rolling Meadows Bowling League lost on their way to the lanes."[30] Fortunately, we also earned a few good friends and supporters on the jury, just as we did in the country as a whole.

30 Lukas' book would be published as *The Barnyard Epithet and Other Obscenities: Notes on the Chicago Conspiracy Trial*. New York: Harper & Row, 1970.

Daily Press Conference

David Fenton Photo

In the 1960s, the "generation gap" was a phrase used to describe a great chasm between people over and under age thirty. Abbie and Jerry liked to say, "You can't trust anyone over thirty." This "generation gap" was especially evident in our federal courtroom. One image of the gap was our two tables in front of the jury. The table for the prosecution featured a law book and a crisp note pad. Their table along with their personal appearance was professional and immaculate. In contrast, we were dressed in sweatshirts and jeans. Abbie and Jerry wore headbands, bright-colored shirts, and beads for pizzazz. Our table was littered with fan mail and candy wrappers and sometimes served as a footrest. On one occasion, a package of marijuana mailed from a Abbie Hoffman fan was opened and the strong-smelling herb spilled out on our table for the jury to see, causing a hilarious exchange between our lawyer and the judge. After one humorous exchange, Bill Kunstler managed to get the judge to grant him the legal authority to remove the pot package placed in the middle of our messy table and take it out of the federal building by assuring the judge that this "unwanted material will go up in smoke tonight."

In other words, we had fun. We were never politically correct. We made faces to show how we really felt. We joked and poked fun at the government's undercover agents who took the stand with their made-up testimony. When we were bored, we read newspapers or napped so we were ready for the tumultuous nights.

When we first spoke in open court to declare our innocence, Jerry Rubin pleaded not guilty with a raised fist. Abbie blew the jury a kiss while Judge Hoffman hastily instructed the jurors to disregard the kiss. We typically refused to rise when the judge entered the courtroom. One morning, Abbie and Jerry arrived in court dressed in judicial robes. At an opportune moment, they took them off, threw them on the floor, and stomped on this "tarnished symbol of American justice" in front of the judge.

Because I looked somewhat "normal," with glasses and short haircut, the media sometimes referred to me as "the boy next door." Reporters could tell I valued the principles of jurisprudence, but when the government replaced due process with witch hunts—when the courtroom agenda was pure political revenge—I spoke up. To maintain courtroom decorum when any defendant spoke up, federal marshals who lined the courtroom looked like football linebackers in a Super Bowl huddle. I got to experience their strength personally when Bobby Seale tried to defend himself while his lawyer was in surgery. Announcing to the court that he had the Constitutional right to defend himself, Bobby Seale would stand up to cross-examine a witness whenever his name was mentioned. With zero tolerance for Bobby's Constitutional rights claim, the judge ordered the marshals to put Bobby back in his seat. That seemed to be marshal code by "excessive force is encouraged by the Judge." The marshals would push Bobby hard into his swivel chair. As the courtroom tension intensely grew, sometimes we would jump between the marshals and Bobby as the jury was hastily rushed from the courtroom. With a stunned press telling this story to a world audience, there was no hiding the fact that Bobby's defending himself was creating physical push back from the marshals and all-out mayhem in front of the jury.

While the trial often had its sober and serious tone, the mood could change on a dime to humor and delightful fun. HBO and other movie producers tried to recreate the courtroom drama on film, but the real-life theatre of the actual trial exceeded all the movie renditions in my opinion. With unpredictable plot turns, escalating drama, eloquent monologues, and moments of sheer comic relief, this trial was both humorous and riveting to everyone but the prosecution and the judge. If the trial had come from the imagination of a Hollywood screenplay writer, he or she would have won the Oscar.

The trial of the century was simply world-class theater.

Eager for daily updates about this unfolding juicy drama, a massive press corps assembled in Chicago from many countries. During lunch breaks, we held a press conference in a packed-to-the-brim federal building press room every day. A trial—hungry global audience wanted to keep abreast of every juicy detail.

In the evenings following the court proceedings, the defendants who had been granted bail spoke at college campuses. I was always impressed by how American students seemed to understand every trial detail. Before reality TV had even been invented, we were the reality TV show capturing the imagination of the country, especially with college and high school students.

Many students traveled across the United States to see our trial in person, but staying up all night on a city sidewalk in the cold of winter was no guarantee you could get a seat the next morning. Students stood outside the federal building in a line that wrapped around the block that started forming around 4:00 p.m. when the trial was ending and I was leaving the courthouse rushing to get to the airport and catch a flight to some college campus. With the one-hour time difference between Chicago and the East Coast, I usually spoke around 9:00 p.m. to audiences from Maine to Florida. I felt bad not having time to hang out with these dedicated visitors who had come such long distances with their sleeping bags and backpack supplies for a chilly Chicago night adventure and only the hope of experiencing the trial.

While the daytime proceedings were mesmerizing, the evenings were simply extraordinary. When I spoke on a campus, an average turnout was 5,000 students. When Abbie and I spoke together, 25,000 gathered in an armory. When the state governor called out the National Guard because I was speaking, a stadium was the venue.

William Kunstler on Campus

David Fenton Photo

Arriving at an airport, I tried to spot my "undercover" police tails first. Since they stood out like a sore thumb, it was not that hard. With dozens of new student friends tagging along, I introduced myself and let the police 'undercover' agents hear "my rules" for the evening. They were welcome to join me for the talk. I handed them the address and schedule of events. I offered to speak with their captain if they needed me to explain why I would disappear when the speech was over. I wanted the agents to know I would be heading for a party and would gladly explain to their commanding officer that it was not their fault when I vanished into thin air.

Rather than feel intimated by undercover police agents who followed me to speeches, I choose to have fun.

In Texas, the San Antonio airport was shut down for my grand arrival. I thought that was an over reaction but it actually happened. All the passengers on my plane were told to get off while I stayed in my seat and the airport was cleared. I walked through an empty airport surrounded by a super excited student host committee who were surrounded themselves by local police assigned to take us with a police escort that included sirens and flashing lights to the crowded stadium. Texas was not typical, however. More often than not, the police preferred to stay out of sight and remain "undercover" when I arrived which was amusing and delightful to watch as well.

Since an audience had been listening to speakers from their own campus for an hour or more before I spoke, I sometimes walked on stage with feet pounding the floor in frenzied anticipation. It rarely worked to ask an audience to calm down either. Instead, it was better to say something that fired everyone up all the more. I would sometimes acknowledge the audience as "the greatest movement in the history of the Earth!" (which they were) or I might say "We can stop the war in Vietnam from this room right here, right now, tonight—if you say we can." That seemed to send the stoked up intensity into a peaking crescendo and after that, the room might calm down so I could speak.

During these extraordinary evening events, I always shared stories about the day's courtroom drama but my talks focused on the war in Vietnam, especially what I had seen with my own eyes. I shared my experiences with the Vietnamese and described the massive U.S. war on this tiny country in Indochina. On several occasions, the American Legion would turn out to protest my talk. An organization dedicated to "promoting national security, patriotism and devotion to veterans," three hundred veterans might be in the audience hissing like leaky radiators. I would ask them whether anyone among them had actually fought in Vietnam. Someone always shouted back and I made sure he had a mic in his hand immediately. What ensued after that was a spellbinding conversation that elicited amazing and sometimes horrific accounts of that soldier's experiences in Vietnam. A hushed and awed audience would listen with growing respect for the soldier. The soldier might not agree with me that supporting our GIs meant bringing them home, but the hissing stopped as the audience and the American Legion realized together that this war was like no other in American history. Millions of Americans, including thousands of Vietnam veterans, were openly opposing this war. That was the reality of our time. Our movement had pushed a national issue into a mainstream awareness. I saw nothing wrong with the Sixties movement claiming the flag of patriotism either, when a majority of the American public supported our call to bring the GIs home.

Today's movement can do the same. Today we are the voice of this country as well, standing up for humanity to take back America.

After the speech came the all-night party. Since I was in my late twenties, late nights were not a problem. It was getting up the next morning that was my challenge. Unfortunately, I had no choice in the matter. Judge Hoffman entered the courtroom at 10:00 a.m. sharp Chicago time. If I was not in the courtroom and in my seat when the Judge arrived, my bail would be revoked, and I would spend the rest of the trial calling Cook County Jail my home behind bars. I had one close call too. My plane was delayed on the East Coast and I arrived at the courtroom fifteen minutes past the perilous deadline. My lawyers understood the gravity of the moment and rose to the occasion with an award-winning shuck and jive legal mumbo jumbo to engage the judge until there was no time left for any more shenanigans. At that exact moment, I walked through the large courtroom doors to gasps in the courtroom. I was eternally grateful to Bill Kunstler for his brilliant performance under the pressure of contempt, bond revoking, and jail for me.

To present the government's case, only government employees were listed on the prosecutor's witness list. I was amazed that these paid government witnesses who claimed to have heard me say words that could convict me would never relay my comments said in public. They always relied on "private conversations"—conversations that were completely fictional too. Made-up testimony was the government's strategy. If you find this hard to believe, I felt the same way at the time. Having sworn they would tell the truth and nothing but the truth, these government witnesses, one by one, gave fabricated fairytales for their testimony.

Some undercover agents let their hair grow long while others put on black biker leather jackets to "infiltrate" our meetings that were open to the public. We never vetted people coming to a gathering of volunteers so when these agents called their participation "infiltration," that was silly It was during those meeting breaks when I was getting coffee or going to the men's room that an undercover agent would supposedly come up to me and have a chat. These talks always took place away from the group where it was just the two of us. While my memory was good, I could never remember having any of these conversations. When the undercover agents described a meeting in the men's room, their account crossed into some parallel universe. Listening to them in the courtroom, I was amazed to hear what I supposedly said in these private two-person converations. I supposedly called for "rock throwing" and "Molotov cocktails." Police officer Robert Pierson was especially prolific at putting words in our mouths. He said Abbie Hoffman told him the demonstrators would break windows if the police pushed them out of Lincoln Park.

Fred Hampton Killed in Bed By Chicago Police While Sleeping

David Fenton Photo

He "overheard" Jerry, Bobby, and me say we would resist the police and employ violence. William Frapolly was another undercover policeman whose testimony was a made up fantasy. He declared, under oath, that he had heard virtually every defendant state his intention to incite confrontations with the police. The government called fifty-three witnesses who swore to tell nothing but the truth—but they didn't. Saddest of all were the Illinois district attorneys who allowed this deception to be presented to an American jury in a federal courtroom while the whole world was watching.

We challenged the court's legitimacy. We called more than 100 witnesses, who ranged from convention delegates who had been beaten or gassed to well-known Sixties personalities like Allen Ginsberg, William Styron, Dick Gregory, Norman Mailer, Arlo Guthrie, and Judy Collins. Musicians and celebrities testified in court about our intent in Chicago. Facing made-up testimony against us and a judge supporting every government motion, it seemed our best strategy was to challenge the legitimacy of the federal courtroom itself.

Whatever the government underhandedly tried to do, our strategy was to bring their real agenda into the light.

Our request to subpoena President Lyndon Johnson was denied but Judge Hoffman did allow Mayor Daley in as a defense witness. While the government objected to every defense question directed at the Mayor and the judge upheld every government objection, Mayor Daley didn't get to say much in open court about his role in denying permits or how he fanned the flames that caused the police riots. During a courtroom break, however, when the Mayor was still on the stand, Abbie suggested the two of them could arm wrestle right then and there to settle the whole affair. Even the Mayor smiled at that suggestion.

Abbie and I were the only defendants to testify. I admit I was feeling a little irritated by government witnesses making up conversations about our intentions before the jury. During the trial, I had also experienced my friend Fred Hampton of the Chicago Black Panther Party being shot and killed by Chicago police while he was sleeping in bed. I watched the chairman of the Black Panther Party, Bobby Seale, chained and gagged in a chair next to me as blood spilled from his lips because he had demanded his right to defend himself in court. I was grateful that Abbie took the witness stand before me. Watching him testify with humor and fun helped me realize there was no reason to be wound up tight as a spring. As Abbie brilliantly demonstrated, a little humor and self-deprecation goes a long way in front of a jury and the world media.

When Abbie took the stand, the judge asked him where he lived. He said he was a citizen of the Woodstock Nation and an orphan of America. When asked to tell the jury where his nation was located, his response was priceless.

THE WITNESS: It is a nation of alienated young people. We carry it around with us as a state of mind in the same way as the Sioux Indians carried the Sioux nation around with them. It is a nation dedicated to cooperation versus competition, to the idea that people should have better means of exchange than property or money, that there should be some other basis for human interaction. It is a nation dedicated to—

THE COURT: Just where it is, that is all.

THE WITNESS: It is in my mind and in the minds of my brothers and sisters. It does not consist of property or material but, rather, of ideas and certain values. We believe in a society—

THE COURT: No, we want the place of residence. Nothing about philosophy or India, sir. Just where you live, if you have a place to live. Now you said Woodstock. In what state is Woodstock?

THE WITNESS: It is in the state of mind, in the mind of myself and my brothers and sisters. It is a conspiracy. Presently, the nation is held captive, in the penitentiaries of the institutions of a decaying system.

MR. WEINGLASS: Now, directing your attention to approximately 6:00 a.m., Wednesday, August 28, do you recall what you were doing?

THE WITNESS: I went to eat. I went with Paul Krassner, Beverly Baskinger, and Anita and four police officers—Paul also had two Chicago police officers following him, as well as the two that were following me. We walked and the four of them would drive along behind us.

MR. WEINGLASS: Could you describe for the jury and the Court what you were wearing at that time?

THE WITNESS: Well, I had cowboy boots, and brown pants and a shirt, and I had a gray felt ranger cowboy type hat down over my eyes, like this.

MR.WEINGLASS: What, if anything, occurred while you were sitting there having breakfast?

THE WITNESS: Well, two policemen came in and said, "We have orders to arrest you. You have something under your hat." So I asked them if they had a search warrant and I said, "Did you check it out with Commander Braasch? Me and him got an agreement"—and they went to check it out with him, while we were eating breakfast.

MR. WEINGLASS: After a period of time, did they come back?

THE WITNESS: They came back with more police officers—there were about four or five patrol cars surrounding the restaurant. The Red Squad cops who had been following us came in the restaurant, four or five police, and they said, "We checked. Now will you take off your hat?" They were stern, more serious about it.

MR. WEINGLASS: What did you do?

THE WITNESS: Well, I lifted up the hat and I went "Bang! Bang!" They grabbed me by the jacket and pulled me across the bacon and eggs and Anita over the table, threw me on the floor and out the door and threw me against the car, and they handcuffed me. I was just eating the bacon and going, "Oink Oink!"

MR. WEINGLASS: Did they tell you why you were being arrested?

THE WITNESS: They said they arrested me because I had the word "Fuck" on my forehead. I had put it on with this magic marker before we left the house...for a couple of reasons. One was that I was tired of seeing my picture in the paper and having newsmen come around, and I know if you got that word on your forehead they ain't going to print your picture in the paper. Secondly, it sort of summed up my attitude about the whole thing—what was going on in Chicago. I like that four letter word—I thought it was kind of holy, actually.

MR. WEINGLASS: Abbie Hoffman, prior to coming to Chicago, from April 1968 on to the week of the Convention, did you enter into an agreement with David Dellinger, John Froines, Tom Hayden, Jerry Rubin, Lee Weiner, or Rennie Davis to come to the city of Chicago for the purpose of encouraging and promoting violence during the Convention week?

THE WITNESS: An agreement?

MR. WEINGLASS: Yes.

THE WITNESS: We couldn't agree on lunch.[31]

---

31 Abbie Hoffman testimony from the Chicago Eight trial was based on trial transcripts.

According to the Chicago press, our chief prosecutor, District Attorney Thomas Foran, had plans to run for Governor of Illinois following our trial. The press speculated that vwhen Foran cross-examined me, he could launch his candidacy for Governor. While that didn't work out as planned, my three-day testimony did give me a rare opportunity to talk about the Vietnam War and say what I felt in front of the jury and the country.

Shortly before I took the stand, the government made an unexpected mistake. A Chicago undercover agent made a fatal departure from the scripted game plan of the government. An agent described to the jury for the first time an actual public talk I had given at the University of Chicago. Unlike the other government testimony that could not be refuted with a third party witness, this time was different. When a government agent said I called for riots at the convention in a public gathering and hundreds of people were sitting in the student auditorium hearing what I actually said, his false testimony gave me our first opportunity to recount our actual reasons for coming to Chicago in open court with the government unable to object.

Here are highlights from that testimony and a small portion of my cross-examination by the District Attorney as well.

MR. WEINGLASS: What is your occupation?

THE WITNESS: Since 1967 my primary work and concern has been ending the war in Vietnam. Until the time of this trial I was the national coordinator for the National Mobilization to End the War in Vietnam.

MR. WEINGLASS: Now, directing your attention to the early evening of November 20, 1967, do you recall where you were on that night?

THE WITNESS: I was at the University of Chicago in an auditorium called Judd Hall. It was a meeting of a group called The Resistance. I was a speaker with Bob Ross and David Harris, who is the husband of Joan Baez.

MR. WEINGLASS: Could you relate now to the Court and jury the words that you spoke, as best you can recall, on that particular night?

THE WITNESS: I began by holding up a small steel ball that was green, about the size of a tennis ball and I said, "This bomb was dropped on a city of 100,000 people, a city called Nam Dinh, which is about sixty-five miles south of Hanoi." I said, "It was dropped by an American fighter jet, an F-105," and that when this bomb exploded over Nam Dinh, about 640 of these round steel balls were spewed into the sky. And I said, "When this ball strikes a building or the ground or blows up in any way, these hammers are released and an explosion occurs which sends out about 300 steel pellets. Now one of these balls," I explained, "was roughly three times the power of an old fashioned hand grenade and with 640 of these bombs going off, you can throw steel pellets over an area about a thousand yards long, and about 250 yards wide. Every living thing exposed in that 1000-yard area from this single bomb, ninety percent of every living thing in that area will die," I said, "whether it's a water buffalo or a water buffalo boy." I said that if this bomb were to go off in this room tonight, everyone in the room would die, but as quickly as we could remove the bodies from the room, we could have another discussion about Vietnam. I said "This bomb would not destroy this lecture podium, it would not damage the walls, the ceiling, the floor." I said, "If it is dropped on a city, it takes life but leaves the institutions. It is the ideal weapon, you see, for the mentality that reasons that life is less precious than property." I said that in 1967, the year that we are in, one out of every two bombs dropped on North Vietnam was this weapon. One out of every two. And in 1967, the American Government told the American public that in North Vietnam it was only bombing steel and concrete. Then I said, "I went to Vietnam not as a representative of the government and not as a member of the military but as an American citizen who was deeply perturbed that we lived in a country where our own government was lying to American people about this war. The U.S. Government claimed to be hitting only military targets. Yet what I saw were pagodas that had been gutted, schoolhouses that had been razed, population centers that had been leveled." Then I said that I am going to the Democratic National Convention because I want the world to know that there are thousands of young people in this country who do not want to see a rigged convention rubber stamp another four years of Lyndon Johnson's war.

MR. WEINGLASS: I show you an object marked D-325 for identification and can you identify that object?

THE WITNESS: Yes. This was the bomb that I brought back from Vietnam.

MR. WEINGLASS: If the Court please, the defense would like to offer into evidence D325, the antipersonnel bomb identified by the witness as the object held by him on the night in question.

MR. FORAN: Your Honor, the Government objects to this exhibit for the following reasons. The Vietnamese war, Your Honor, has nothing whatsoever to do with the charges in this indictment. The Vietnamese war, which is a major difficulty of this country and a major concern of every citizen in this country, has nothing whatever to do with whether or not people in the United States have a right to travel in interstate commerce to incite a riot. The methods and techniques of warfare have nothing whatever to do with that charge. The methods and techniques of the seeking of the end of the Vietnam War have nothing to do with the charges of this indictment. The very purpose of the governmental system of the United States is to handle in a purposeful way within the Constitution of the United States the disposition of such complex and difficult and tragic problems that this nation has lived with for about two hundred years. The charges in this indictment, Your Honor, have nothing to do with this type of testimony or this kind of concept, and for that reason, Your Honor, the Government objects.

THE COURT: Objection sustained.

MR. KUNSTLER: Your Honor, at this point I would like to move for a mistrial.

THE COURT: I deny the motion.

MR. RUBIN: You haven't heard it yet.

THE COURT: Oh, there is no ground for a mistrial.

MR. KUNSTLER: But, Your Honor—

THE COURT: I direct the marshal to have this man sit down.

MR. KUNSTLER: Every time I make a motion am I going to be thrown in my seat when I argue it?

MR. DELLINGER: Force and violence. The judge is inciting a riot by asking the marshal to have him sit down.

THE COURT: That man's name is Dellinger?

MARSHAL JONESON: Will you be quiet, Mr. Dellinger?

MR. DELLINGER: After such hypocrisy I don't particularly feel like being quiet. I said before the judge was the chief prosecutor, and he's proved the point.

THE COURT: Will you remain quiet? Will you remain quiet, sir?

MR. DELLINGER: You let Foran give a foreign policy speech, but when he tries to answer it, you interrupt him and won't let him speak. There's no pretense of fairness in this court. All you're doing is employing a riot—employing force and violence to try to keep me quiet. Just like you gagged Bobby Seale because you couldn't afford to listen to the truth that he was saying to you. You're accusing me. I'm a pacifist.

MARSHAL JONESON: Sit down, please, and be quiet.

MR. DELLINGER: I am employing nonviolence, and you're accusing me of violence, and you have a man right here, backed up by guns, jails, and force and violence. That is the difference between us.

MARSHAL JONESON: Will you sit down?

(applause)

THE COURT: Will you continue, please, with the direct examination of this witness?

MR. DELLINGER: There goes the violence right there.

MR. KUNSTLER: That's the Government in operation, Your Honor, as it has been throughout this trial.

THE WITNESS: Your Honor, that's my sister they are taking out of the courtroom.

THE COURT: Even your sister—

MR. RUBIN: Bill, they are taking out my wife.

(cries of "Hey, stop it!")

MR. KUNSTLER: Your Honor, must we always have this, the force and power of the Government?

MR. FORAN: Your Honor—

MR. RUBIN: They are dragging out my wife—will you please—

THE COURT: We must have order in the courtroom.

MR. FORAN: Your Honor, traditionally in American law, cases are tried in a courtroom by the participants in the trial, not the audience, not spectators, not by shouting and screaming. This is the American judicial system, and it's worked very well for two hundred years, and it's not going to change now for these people.

MR. DELLINGER: Yes, it [the system] kept the black people in slavery for two hundred years and wiped out the Indians, and kept the poor people in problems and started the war in Vietnam which is killing off at least a hundred Americans and a thousand Vietnamese every week, and we are trying to stop it.

MARSHAL JONESON: Sit down.

MR. DELLINGER: And you call that ranting and raving and screaming because we speak the truth.

MARSHAL JONESON: Mr. Dellinger, sit down, please.

MR. FORAN: Your Honor, in the American system there is a proper way to raise such issues and to correct them.

MR. DELLINGER: That was the proper way with Fred Hampton, wasn't it?

MR. FORAN: And to correct them, Your Honor, by the proper governmental system, and there is a proper way to do that.

MR. KUNSTLER: Mr. Rubin's wife was thrown out of the courtroom, and he is a defendant here. We would like her returned to the courtroom.

THE COURT: No. As long as the marshals are in charge of the behavior of spectators in this courtroom, they will determine who misbehaves.

MR. RUBIN: Am I entitled to a public trial?

THE COURT: No—you have a public trial.

MR. RUBIN: Does a public trial include my wife being in the courtroom? Am I entitled to a public trial?

THE COURT: I don't talk to defendants who have a lawyer.

MR. RUBIN: You didn't listen to my lawyer, so I have to speak. Am I entitled to a public trial?

THE COURT: You may continue with the direct examination of this witness. If you don't, I will just have to ask him to get off the witness stand.

MR. WEINGLASS: Your Honor, the witness has seen from his vantage point his sister forcibly taken from this room. I wonder if we could have a short recess to resolve that?

THE COURT: No recess. No, no. There will be no recess, sir. You will proceed to examine this witness.

* * *

THE COURT: Is there any cross-examination of this witness?

MR. FORAN: You did tell people...that if the police kept the demonstrators in the park and they couldn't get out, that you had an easy solution for it: "just riot." That's what you said, didn't you?

THE WITNESS: I have never in all my life said that to riot was an easy solution to anything, ever.

MR. FORAN: And you sat here in this courtroom and you heard Officer Bock and Dwayne Oklepek and Officer Frapolly testify to all of these things, didn't you?

THE WITNESS: I listened to your speices testify about us, yes, sir and it was a grace to me. I hope after this trail you can properly respond, Mr. Foran. I really do. I hope we have that chance.

MR. FORAN: I don't know what he is—what are you—

THE WITNESS: That you and I can sit down and talk about what happened in Chicago and why it happened.

THE COURT: Mr. Witness—

THE WITNESS: I would like to do that very much.

THE COURT: Mr. Witness—

MR. FORAN: Your Honor—

THE COURT: Do you hear me, sir?

THE WITNESS: Yes, I do.

THE COURT: You didn't—

THE WITNESS: I am sorry.

THE COURT: You paid no attention to me. I direct you not to make any volunteered observations. I have made this order several times during your testimony.

THE WITNESS: I apologize.

THE COURT: I do not accept your apology, sir.

MR. FORAN: You and your people wanted to have violence in Lincoln Park, didn't you?

THE WITNESS: No, sir. We wanted to avoid violence.

MR. FORAN: You wanted it for one purpose. You wanted it for the purpose of discrediting the Government of the United States; isn't that correct?

THE WITNESS: I wanted to discredit the Government's policies by bringing a half million Americans to Chicago at the time of the Convention.

MR. FORAN: Have you ever said that you came to Chicago to display a growing militant defiance of the authority of the government?

THE WITNESS: I don't recall saying that.

MR. FORAN: Could you have said it?

THE WITNESS: Well, that would be out of context. I would talk about the war. I would talk about racism.

MR. FORAN: Have you ever said it in context or out of context?

THE WITNESS: But the context is all-important, don't you see? It is most important.

MR. FORAN: Not in a statement like that. Have you ever said that?

THE WITNESS: I don't recall ever saying that.

MR. FORAN: And you wanted violence at the International Amphitheatre also, didn't you?

THE WITNESS: Just the opposite.

MR. FORAN: Isn't it a fact that you wanted violence in order to impose an international humiliation on the people who ruled this country? Isn't that a fact?

THE WITNESS: It is my belief that it was you who wanted the violence, Mr. Foran, not me.

MR. FORAN: Your Honor, may that be stricken, and may I have the question answered?

THE COURT: Certainly, the statement may go out. The witness is directed to be careful about his answers. Please read the question for the witness.

(*question read*)

THE WITNESS: I did not want violence, Mr. Foran.

MR. FORAN: You did want to impose an international humiliation on the people who ruled this country; isn't that correct?

THE WITNESS: I am afraid that our government has already humiliated itself in the world community, sir.

MR. FORAN: That the purpose of your meeting in Chicago was to impose an international humiliation on the people who rule this country, to display a growing militant defiance of the authority of the Government, to paralyze the "magnificent mile" of Michigan Avenue. You have said all of those things, haven't you, that that was your purpose in coming to Chicago and that you achieved it?

THE WITNESS: No, I never indicated that that was our purpose in coming to Chicago.

MR. FORAN: Now, have you and Mr. Hayden stated in this "Politics After Chicago" that since the institutions of this country cannot be changed from within, the people will take to the streets? Have you stated that?

THE WITNESS: Yes. I wish you would read the whole context.

MR. FORAN: You have stated that, have you not?

THE WITNESS: Yes.

MR. FORAN: You have stated, "We learned in Chicago what it means to declare that the streets belong to the people."

THE WITNESS: Yes.

MR. FORAN: Did you state that the battle line is no longer drawn in the obscure paddies of Vietnam or the dim ghetto streets, but is coming closer to suburban sanctuaries and corporate board rooms? The gas that fell on us in Chicago also fell on Hubert? The street that was paralyzed was the "magnificent mile" of Michigan Avenue?

THE WITNESS: Yes. That is quite different from what you said before.

MR. FORAN: You have stated that your program is to discredit the authority of the Government, which is deaf to its own system, and railroad an election through America as if Vietnam were the caboose?

THE WITNESS: Boy, that's right on.

MR. FORAN: You stated that, did you not, that you wanted to discredit the authority of a Government, which is deaf to its own citizens?

THE WITNESS: Well, I embrace those words. I don't know if I said them, but those words are just right.

MR. FORAN: Have you ever stated in the words that I have asked you, "We won the Battle of Chicago"? Have you ever said that in any context?

THE WITNESS: You are not interested in the context, I suppose.

MR. FORAN: In any context, Mr. Davis.

THE WITNESS: Yes, I believe we won the battle in Chicago.

MR. FORAN: That your program would include press conferences, disruptions, and pickets dramatizing whatever demands you wanted?

THE WITNESS: Yes, I believe that contest that will shape the political character in the next decade was really shaped in Chicago in the context between the Daleys and the Nixons, and... the Reagans and the young people who expressed their hopes in the streets in Chicago. And I think, frankly, in that context, it is going to be clear it is not the Daleys, or the Humphreys, or the Johnsons who are the future of this country. We are the future of this country.

MR. FORAN: Isn't it a fact that you have said, Mr. Davis, that the Battle of Chicago continues today? The war is on. The reason we are here tonight is to try to figure out how we are going to get the kind of mutiny that Company A started in South Vietnam and spread it to every army base, every high school, every community in this country. That is what you said about the Battle of Chicago continuing today, isn't it? Isn't it a fact that you have said, "If we go about our own work, and if we make it clear that there can be no peace in the United States until every soldier is brought out of Vietnam and this imperialistic system is destroyed." Have you said that?

THE WITNESS: I don't recall those exact words, but those certainly are my sentiments, that we should not rest until this war is over and until the system—

MR. FORAN: And until this imperialistic system is destroyed?

THE WITNESS: Until the system that made that war is changed, the foreign policy.

MR. FORAN: The way you decided to continue the Battle of Chicago, the way you decided to fight the Battle of Chicago, was by incitement to riot, wasn't it?

THE WITNESS: No, sir, by organizing, by organizing within the army, within high schools, within factories and communities across this country.

MR. FORAN: By inciting to riot within high schools, and within colleges, and within factories, and within the army, isn't that right, sir?

THE WITNESS: No. No, sir. No, I am trying to find a way that this generation can make this country something better than what it has been.

MR. FORAN: Your Honor, he is no longer responding to the question.

THE COURT: I strike the answer of the witness and direct the jury to disregard it.

MR. FORAN: And what you want to urge young people to do is to revolt, isn't that right?

THE WITNESS: Yes, revolt.

MR. FORAN: And you have stated, have you not, "That there can be no question by the time that I am through that I have every intention of urging that you revolt, that you join the Movement, that you become a part of a growing force for insurrection in the United States." You have said that, haven't you?

THE WITNESS: I was standing right next to Fred Hampton when I said that, who was murdered in this city by policemen.

MR. FORAN: Your Honor, I move to strike that.

THE COURT: Yes, the answer may certainly go out. The question is wholly unrelated to one Fred Hampton.

MR. FORAN: Wouldn't it be wonderful, Your Honor, if the United States accused people of murder as these people do without proof, without trial, and without any kind of evidence having been presented in any kind of a decent situation?

MR. KUNSTLER: A man is murdered in his bed, while he is sleeping, by the police.

MR. FORAN: I have no further cross-examination.

THE COURT: Redirect examination.

MR. WEINGLASS: Redirect is unnecessary, Your Honor.[32]

* * *

For five and a half months, a federal judge in a Chicago courtroom ruled in favor of the government. Eight defendants were denied access to government evidence obtained without a warrant. Documents we wrote stating our intentions for nonviolent demonstrations in Chicago were barred from evidence. The judge

32 Rennie Davis testimony from the Chicago Eight trial was taken from trial transcripts.

barred former Attorney General Ramsey Clark from testifying about his opposition to the prosecution of the demonstrators as well. The judge also limited our ability to question Mayor Daley. For these and other reasons, it seemed our best and only option was to paint our defense landscape from a palette of common sense, verbal resistance, and an edge of humor and fun.

We regularly asked the judge to rule on questions that made fun of the court. We profusely protested when we brought a birthday cake to court and the marshals "arrested Bobby Seale's birthday cake." We pounded our feet on the floor when we needed a bathroom break as our lawyer petitioned the court for a fifteen-minute break, knowing our motion to break for the men's room would always be denied. We asked the judge whether musicians who came to Chicago could sing the songs they performed at our festival of life in Lincoln Park on the witness stand.

Every day there was a new courtroom drama but none compared to the one event that ignited the anger of the world's public with the chaining and gagging of Bobby Seale in open court.

When Bobby's lawyer could not participate in the trial because of his surgery, Bobby Seale argued that he had the constitutional right to defend himself. When his motion to Judge Hoffman was denied, he pointed to the pictures of the nation's founding fathers behind the judge's chair to remind Judge Hoffman that they were slave owners and the judge was behaving in that same tradition today. Marshals tried to keep Bobby from speaking and used physical force to push him into his seat when he stood up to question a witness. While the force used in a public courtroom was shocking, I never got over the day Bobby Seale was carried into the room chained to his chair with a pressure bandage wrapped around his head and mouth to keep him from speaking. His head wrap never worked either. Bobby kept calling out in front of the jury with his muffled voice, "I demand my constitutional right to defend myself." Each day as the drama unfolded, the head wrappings to quiet Bobby got more padded and tightly bound, but nothing could stop him from speaking. He could always be heard behind his thick pressure bandages.

Bobby Seale was heard in Asia, Africa, Europe, South and Central America, Canada, and the United States. A black man, chained and gagged in an American courtroom for defending himself, became a world symbol of our trial. Eventually, Bobby was severed from the trail of the rest of us and the press started calling us the Chicago Seven. For us, however, we were always the Chicago Eight. Bobby was supposed to be re-tried by the government at another time, but he never was. Instead, he won the hearts and minds of people around the world with his courage and grit in a Chicago federal courtroom. When Bobby Seale was chained and gagged, he gave new meaning and pride to the phrase "power to the people."

When the time came for the jury to decide on our guilt or innocence, the jurors were divided and deadlocked—no different than the country itself. Many Americans perceived us as citizens who opposed an unjust war but got stripped of our First Amendment rights. Others felt we had undermined the country by opposing the war and forcing the police to act against us. After a lengthy jury deliberation, the jury communicated to the judge that they were deadlocked. Infuriated by the decision, the judge told the foreman that "too much time and money were devoted for such a decision." The jurors had to go back and deliberate until they decided. Since the jurors had been sequestered for five and a half months and were unable to see their families, it seemed their only way to leave their hotel rooms was to compromise. And that's what they did. They found us guilty of one charge and innocent of the other.

When the jury foreman read the verdict, Weiner and Froines were innocent of all charges. Dellinger, Hayden, Hoffman, Rubin, and I were guilty of the anti-riot law, but innocent of the conspiracy charge. The judge gave us the maximum five year penalty. During the time the jury was deliberating, Judge Hoffman also sentenced us to prison time for "contempt of court." I was charged with twenty-three counts of contempt and sentenced to more than two years in prison. Our lawyer, Bill Kunstler, was sentenced to four years as an officer of the court for his "contempt" of court when defending us.

After our sentencing, we were hustled into waiting vans and driven to the Cook County Jail where we were separated from each other. I was shuffled into a large room with 300 prisoners, one of whom was a twenty-two-year-old black resident of Chicago's Southside who helped me find a bunk bed. As we walked to a cell room, he asked me my name. "Rennie," I said. "Rennie who?" "Rennie Davis," I replied. And with that, pandemonium filled the cell block. Surrounded by shouting, cheering inmates who had followed the trial every day, I was lifted onto a table while outside the prison, 20,000 people had gathered and were chanting for our release. The night of our arrest, 10,000 towns and cities across the United States erupted. People sat down in busy streets blocking traffic. Students marched and organized candlelight vigils. In Santa Barbara, a dumpster was set on fire and pushed through the doors of the Bank of America. Our movement was on fire and American students were angry.

1969 Protest to Resistance

Days of Rage

David Fenton Photo

1969 Protest to Resistance

People's Park

David Fenton Photo

1970 Protest to Resistance

Nixon Counter-Inaugural
David Fenton Photo

The other prison inmates—nearly all of them black and most of them waiting in jail for trial for nine to twelve months because they could not post a $100 bond—would have to stay in prison when we got bailed out. Knowing our staff was fundraising to raise our bail, I asked one of the guards enthralled with the Chicago Seven to communicate with the other defendants. "Let's stay in prison and raise money to bail everyone else out when we leave." The Chicago 7 agreed and we spent two extra weeks in solitary confinement while our staff raised bond money for the other Cook County inmates.

Looking back on the Chicago trial, I have many fond memories but my final evening at a celebration of mothers, fathers, and their bailed-out sons, hugging and toasting the Chicago 7 throughout the night at a South Side restaurant was special. The restaurant owner joined our party and proudly announced dinner was on the house. It was a moving closing ceremony for the "trial of the century."

With the resistance movement growing in the United States, the U.S. Court of Appeals reversed our contempt convictions and remanded them for retrial.

In the retrial, the government dropped all charges but two against me. With the first charge, Judge Edward Gignoux ruled that my remarks to the jury while Bobby Seale was bound and gagged had not caused a decorum breakdown. The Judge said the trial disruption had come from "the appalling spectacle of a bound and gagged defendant along with the marshal's effort to subdue him." Certain contempt charges against Dellinger, Rubin, Hoffman, and Kunstler were upheld, but no one was sentenced to jail or fined. On the issue of retrying the Chicago Seven, the Department of Justice was wary—I think wisely—not to try us again for our "crimes" of free speech in Chicago.

Chapter 6

LESSONS AND TRIUMPHS

Vietnam and America

As our movement shifted from protest to resistance, nine hundred and eighty-one Vietnam U.S. servicemen missing in action had families who were resisting as well. The Vietnamese had not released the names of U.S. prisoners of war and no international agency had inspected Vietnam's POW prison camps. U.S. military families were enraged by the shroud of secrecy and utterly rejected the Vietnamese claim that the U.S. invasion was a war crime and that American POWs were treated humanely.

Vietnamese history was not required reading in American colleges. The successive foreign invasions throughout Vietnam's past were largely unknown in the West. A tradition that held the government of a foreign power invading their country should not be recognized was rarely discussed in American law schools.

A Vietnamese tradition held that the citizens who lived in the invading country were not the enemy. When the "peace sentiment" would slowly emerge among the citizens who lived in the invading country, the organization or coalition that best represented that sentiment should be recognized by Vietnam as the voice of the invading country. Since our anti-war coalition was the largest in the United States, the Vietnamese decided any U.S. POW releases should be made to our coalition and not to the U.S. Government.

In a gesture to the families of captured U.S. servicemen, Vietnam first decided to release the POW names to an "American representative." I was asked to go to Paris to receive the names from the North Vietnamese ambassador to France. After clearing customs, I visited an ornate French government building with a massive—and I mean massive—stately hall where I was greeted by the Vietnamese ambassador to France, who met me in this great hall and presented me with the list of names of American

POWs. I immediately turned them over to the office of Senator Edward Kennedy. Afterwards, I spoke to an international press corps that had an intense interest in this unusual gesture. Since I was in no position to evaluate the list or say whether it was accurate or complete, I played a small bit in a big drama.

Later, however, the North Vietnamese Government made another gesture. This time, they wanted to release a POW delegation to me because of my role in our coalition. Several months before the start of the Chicago trial, a telegram arrived at my apartment, inviting me to come to Vietnam and bring American POWs home. I knew the United States had no formal relations with North Vietnam and no extradition treaty existed between our two countries. That meant I would need travel approval from Judge Hoffman for such a trip. The State Department dispatched a high ranking official from Washington to present the government's position to the court—bringing American POWs back to the United States was in our national interest.

In my first ever encounter with Judge Hoffman, I realized that national interest hardly mattered to him at all. I was stunned when he flat-out denied the State Department request, saying I would probably never return from Hanoi to Chicago to stand trial. Perhaps he imagined I would slip into the jungles of Vietnam and disappear forever. Judge Hoffman denied my motion to bring American POWs home to their families. My attorneys with the State Department representative bolted out his courtroom and rushed to the U.S. Court of Appeals. Forty-five minutes later, Judge Otto Kerner reversed Judge Hoffman's decision.

With court approval, I was on my way to Vietnam to bring POWs back to their families.

I boarded a plane with a delegation of anti-war activists—Linda Evans, Grace Paley, and James Johnson along with filmmakers Robert Kramer, Norman Fruchter, and John Douglas. The filmmakers had been granted a rare opportunity to film Ho Chi Minh, who wanted to speak to the American public on television. Unfortunately, the President of Vietnam was not in good health and was unable to conduct the interview after we arrived.

Between my first trip and second trip to Vietnam, two years of antiwar mobilizations, and shifting public opinion had largely discredited every U.S. claim about the Vietnam War. News reports routinely debunked the official reasons our government asserted for waging this war and GIs were publically sharing their accounts of how their military command had turned excessively dangerous to U.S. ground troops conducting the war as well. A bedrock of American patriotism—my country, right or wrong—was being challenged by American GIs themselves who had been forced by commanders to commit horrific crimes, including the murder of women and children.

Our anti-war movement was growing by leaps and bounds with the support of this public ground swell. Even people who did not support our tactics of mass mobilizations tended to agree with our position to bring the troops home. As the Vietnam War consumed the nightly attention of American television audiences, the U.S. Government kept painting itself into a corner. U.S. commanders seemed to constantly miscalculate the strength of the Vietnamese resistance with ruinous consequences. The world's leading military superpower seemed unable to grasp the history and determination of this tiny Southeast Asian culture.

Even when American public opinion turned decisively against the Democratic Party for conducting the war, the newly-elected Republican government refused to align with the majority of public opinion. Instead, President Nixon doubled down on his conviction that he would never "lose a war" on his watch.

Today, thoughtful Americans looking back on this history see the mistakes made by our government Historians have documented how the State Department, Defense Department, and White House miscalculated the Vietnamese at nearly every stage of the escalation. Even when the U.S. Embassy in Saigon was militarily overrun, and the American military was literally driven out of South Vietnam in a humiliating defeat, the American command struggled to understand how it was possible. No one in the State Department seemed to remember that Vietnamese mobilizations against "superior" invaders had characterized invasions of Vietnam throughout the centuries. The Pentagon was certain that a peasant Third World country could never defeat the United States of America. No government official could imagine the nightmare of January 30, 1968 when Vietnam showed the world once again it could mobilize hundreds of thousands of warriors in a massive coordinated attack against an advanced foreign power.

In Vietnam's first major countrywide offensive against the United States military, the hallmarks of its previous historic mobilizations were on full public display. In the thirteenth century, a Mongol emperor ordered a half-million troops to invade Vietnam. It took Vietnam thirty years to defeat that army, but it did. The emperor lost his entire navy in a surprise attack at Ha Long Bay. Today, West Point students study the classic 1954 battle of Dien Bien Phu when the mortifying defeat of the French military occurred. In that historic battle, the Vietnamese moved heavy equipment over "impossible" mountain passes before digging tunnels under an open field until the Viet Minh were directly beneath an "invincible" French fortress. That's how the Vietnamese defeated the French. The 1968 Tet Offensive against the U.S. followed the footsteps of that long tradition.

Vietnam's first large offensive during the American war did not end the war—that came later—but it was the largest Vietnamese military mobilization up to that point. It shocked the U.S. military and confused the American public. Like previous Vietnamese mobilizations, the 1968 assault seemed to come out of nowhere with coordinated attacks on more than one hundred towns and cities simultaneously throughout South Vietnam. Both the U.S. military and the American public were stunned.

Tet is a traditional national Vietnamese holiday to celebrate the New Year. To support soldier morale in South Vietnam, Saigon's President Thieu announced a thirty-six-hour Tet recreational leave for half his forces. Neither Washington nor Saigon showed any awareness that an offensive was brewing. American intelligence officers were enjoying themselves at a Saigon pool party the evening of the Tet Offensive. When the highly coordinated battle was over, Secretary of Defense Clark Clifford, described the U.S. military as "approaching panic." General Westmoreland spoke with the media about the offensive in full denial. Only his closest associates acknowledged the commanding general was also stunned that the Vietnamese could coordinate so many attacks at one time in secrecy. While history has shown this type of miscalculation was the pattern during previous Vietnamese invasions, the U.S. State Department felt no need to learn the lessons of history.

Before the Tet Offensive, our government's approach to smoothing over the growing anxiety of a war-weary public was to promote upbeat public relations campaigns. As the Johnson

White House watched public support for the war slipping away, public relations campaigns like the "Success Offensive" were shamelessly launched. The public relations goal was to convince the public that the U.S. military was winning the war. To beat the drums for the Success Offensive, Vice President Hubert Humphrey went on television to declare "We are on the offensive. Territory is being gained. We are making steady progress." "Pacification" director Ellsworth Bunker released a statement that claimed 68 percent of the South Vietnamese population was under the control of Saigon, and only 17 percent was under the control of the South Vietnamese resistance fighters called the Viet Cong. One prominent U.S. field commander bragged that "the Viet Cong have been defeated."[33]

Over time, the public grew weary of these announcements and mostly responded with a wait-and-see attitude. Before the Tet Offensive, General Westmoreland boasted that he hoped the communists would launch an attack "because we are looking for a fight." When he got his fight in a one hundred cities at the same time, it made him look ridiculous to anyone paying attention.

I am not saying the Vietnamese preparations for the Tet Offensive were never noticed by American intelligence. By January, 1968, U.S. official estimates showed the opposition forces based in South Vietnam totaled 323,000 men and were organized into nine divisions. Given America's vast military superiority, however, the assessment of U.S. intelligence was always the same. The "enemy" was incapable of any large-scale general offensive. One intelligence analyst acknowledged that if U.S. commanders had seen the Vietnamese's entire Tet battle plan before it was launched, they would still not have believed it. No matter the evidence or the fact that Vietnam had a long tradition of defeating foreign invaders, the United States remained unwavering in its self-deception. The result for the United States was just as ruinous as it had been for the other nations that had invaded Vietnam through the centuries.[34]

On my second visit to Vietnam, I wanted to understand how this was possible. How could a developing peasant nation subjected to massive aerial bombing and 500,000 U.S. "boots on the

33 This summary of "The Tet Offensive" is largely drawn from Wikipedia, the free encyclopedia, https://en.wikipedia.org/wiki/Tet_Offensive, and from This Day in History, January 30, 1968, "Tet Offensive Shakes Cold War Confidence."

34 Ibid.

ground" mount major offensives against the world's military superpower? Was it conceivable that the Vietnamese could win this war militarily?

It was my feeling that the panhandle region of Vietnam located between the nineteenth and seventeenth parallels might hold some answers. Though the purpose of my second trip was to bring American POWs home to their families, I wanted to visit the panhandle and see for myself.

In April, 1968, President Johnson announced the U.S. military was "limiting the bombing." The public welcomed the announcement without realizing that "limitation" meant that U.S. sorties would be stopped in the northern two-thirds of North Vietnam, while the Seventh Fleet secretly stepped up the air war by concentrating its bombing almost entirely on North Vietnam's tiny panhandle region. Blocking the flow of supplies and troops to the South through this tiny narrow region of Vietnam was the new military strategy. Having read some of the statistics on the number of bombs dropped, I could not imagine how an urban center like the city of Vinh survived such round-the-clock pounding by U.S. fighter jets. U.S. fight jets dropped more bombs on this tiny corner of the world than the total tonnage of World War II and Korea combined. While the American public was told the U.S. bombing of North Vietnam had been "limited", the U.S. military actually doubled its air strikes while radically narrowing its target area.

No one from the Western world had traveled to the panhandle between the nineteenth and seventeenth parallels since this unprecedented bombing assault began. Facing the considerable hurdles of making such a trip, I did not think it would happen. I knew it was dangerous. After a long deliberation, however, our hosts said yes—that we could visit the panhandle.

I traveled from Hanoi to the seventeenth parallel wondering how anyone living in the panhandle could have survived. I was especially curious to see the "gateway to the south"—the city of Vinh—once a center of revolutionary activity in earlier centuries that had developed into an industrial center during the French occupation. To hear U.S. pilots tell it, the city had been bombed back to the "stone age." I had images of Hamburg or Dresden after those cities were carpet bombed during World War II. In those devastations, a structure might have one wall standing. A person could speculate that a destroyed building had once been a factory. Vinh more closely resembled the moon with crater upon crater, like the aftermath of an atom bomb without the radiation.

While the city was gone, the Vietnamese who lived in the city seemed to have missed the largest aerial assault in history.

A smiling parade of energetic people had dug into the Earth to set up living quarters inside a deep tunnel system. Squeezing my Western size body through one of these narrow passageways was a feat in overcoming claustrophobia but a marvel to see. After I entered one of the underground corridors, it opened into a large cavernous space deep in the Earth where I watched a resilient performance of women singing and dancing for a free and independent Vietnam. In panhandle "basement" theaters like this one, Vietnam's culture seemed buoyant and passionate, despite the unimaginable bombardment from the sky.

With the end of the war and the passage of decades, the American public slowly learned that Vietnam was not our enemy after all. Now that the Vietnam war is over, can we finally let ourselves acknowledge what actually happened?

Long before the United States sent troops to South Vietnam, the North Vietnamese were in a full preparation mode to survive their country's destruction. They saw what was coming and got prepared. As today's movement realizes what is coming in the present time—the harsh consequences of how we live on this planet—our movement can get prepared as well. We can benefit by learning how Vietnam did it.

Understanding a people's war like Vietnam's, we get to appreciate what it looks like when every citizen becomes involved and every village, street, and plant becomes self-sufficient like a decentralized fortress. In North Vietnam, entire cities moved to the countryside before the bombing began. During my first visit to Vietnam, Hanoi's population had already reduced to half its normal size. Once today's movement realizes that climate change is coming, we can have the wisdom to set up thriving, self-sufficient, de-centralized communities in preparation as well. That's when Vietnam will become interesting to study and understand.

Vietnam's entire economy was decentralized. Large factories were relocated to caves or small rural villages. In the panhandle region, people built super-deep tunnels early on. When food shortages became widespread, people shared whatever they had—and supported each other like family. When a bridge was destroyed, it was quickly replaced by dirt fords or ferries that were durable, easily repaired, and nearly impossible to stop. In the panhandle region, I saw Vietnam's amazing foresight, resilient spirit and cohesive culture with my own eyes.

Since a global storm is coming to our own time and the New Humanity movement has time to prepare, the value of setting up and getting ready before the great seismic shift arrives may be the greatest gift we can give ourselves.

The Vietnamese did not wait and see to understand what was about to happen. Long before the U.S. bombing of Vietnam began, the nation of Vietnam had the foresight to prepare. As early as 1965, when U.S. troops were first deployed to Vietnam, nearly 500,000 Vietnamese had already organized into networks that could repair bomb destruction in the north before the bombing had even started. Supply trains and truck convoys were organized early on as well so they could operate from small units that traveled only at night. Trucks and equipment were available to haul supplies, but it was carts, wheelbarrows, and two baskets on a pole carried by peasant women that were widely employed.

Just like Vietnam, The New Humanity can also have the foresight to sense what is coming and the wisdom to prepare with local, self-sufficient, united communities that can live and thrive while resiliently adapting in the midst of epic change. Our future depends on it. Just because our government was unable to comprehend the resiliency of Vietnam's ancient culture did not mean the Sixties movement had to put its blinders on too. Just because today's civilization cannot understand how we live on Earth has consequences—that harsh lessons are coming—doesn't mean today's movement cannot figure it out and get ready now.

While a Vietnamese military victory was considered "impossible" to our Pentagon, the Vietnamese did, in fact, mobilize the most advanced guerrilla force in modern history. No media network ever fully explained to the American public why ordinary Vietnamese were willing to pay any price to defend their homeland. The

American public was told these were "Vietnamese communists" that had to be "contained" to secure "The Free World." Only the anti-war movement including thousands of antiwar GIs stationed in Vietnam seemed to realize that the people of Vietnam were not our enemy. We figured it out long before the United States "normalized" its relations with Vietnam decades later and decided to court Vietnam to join an Asian alliance to help balance the rise of China.

Movements do figure things out when governments cannot. We have done it before and we can do it again.

When the Vietnam War ended on April 29, 1975, a U.S. helicopter was barely able to lift off in time to escape from the roof of the American Embassy. For every person who escaped that final blistering offensive, a thousand more did not get out. The world's military superpower was humiliated and the Vietnamese Saigon military was routed into the jungles of Cambodia where it camped out in hardship for years.

What happened in South Vietnam following the American defeat was horrific for the Vietnamese whose only "crime" was living in a South Vietnamese city and turning to the Saigon government for support. After the American war, millions of Vietnamese fled Vietnam to live in exile. Many who could not get out were imprisoned or "reeducated" or tortured.

Like the U.S. Civil War, healing the wounds of war in Vietnam has been slow and painful for many Vietnamese who had to flee their country.

I returned to Hanoi from the panhandle in time for the twentieth anniversary of the Geneva Convention—the international conference that followed the Vietnamese defeat of the French. Every foreign ambassador stationed in Hanoi was in attendance. I sat midway in a large auditorium as Pham Van Dong, the Prime Minister of North Vietnam, walked onto the stage. Unexpectedly, with every curious eye following him, he descended into the audience, walked past the seated diplomats, and stopped in front of me. "How's your head? How's your head?" he exclaimed, excitedly patting the top of his own head. For a moment, I was unsure what he meant until it dawned on me he had seen an Associated Press photo of me when my head was wrapped in a pressure bandage the day I stood on that upside down wastebasket in front of the Conrad Hilton. Grinning back, I assured the Prime Minister that my head was fine, but that some people thought I should have my head examined traveling all this distance to visit the moonscape of Vietnam's panhandle. He laughed with me and gave me five minutes to share what I saw with my own eyes—the hell of war blooming with a human spirit that could not be dampened by the greatest avalanche of bombs in history.

After our U.S. delegation attended a final ceremony with our Vietnamese hosts, three American POWs were released from prison to us—Navy pilot Lt. Robert F. Frishman, Seaman Douglas B. Hegdahl, and Air Force Captain Wesley L. Rumble. We left Hanoi for Vientiane, Laos, on August 5, 1969. No public statements were made until we reached New York City. While U.S. military officers boarded our plane in Vientiane, they stayed sequestered in the back during the long flight to New York. When we landed, they took control of the three servicemen and gave them time with their families before the released POWs made brief statements to the press.

I met with the media separately and reporters were desperate to know the conditions of all the captured prisoners. They demanded an account of the servicemen missing in action as well. Since I had not seen any POW prison myself, I could not describe prison conditions or answer questions about servicemen missing in action.

I had experienced mad dog press hysteria before but nothing compared with New York City's media frenzy that day.

When Lt. Frishman spoke to the media, he selected his words cautiously. He was "happy to be returning home, to be back with my country and my wife." To the American press, I was cautious too. I could only say what I saw. American POWs shot down in Vietnam were back in the United States with their families, and the antiwar movement had played a part in helping it happen.

While these Sixties stories happened for me, everyone who participated in the Sixties movement has their extraordinary stories too. They live in your family. They are your neighbors down the street. You should talk to them as well. They will gladly share their memories, too. I suggest it will be worth your time to speak with them if you're thinking about joining today's movement yourself.

Should they happen to bring out their photographs of Woodstock, Chicago, Haight-Ashbury, or other iconic images of the Sixties, be prepared for one picture especially. Taken at Kent State University in Ohio by a student, it became one of the iconic images of an unarmed college student lying dead, face-down on the ground, killed by the Ohio National Guard as a friend screamed with anguish over his dead body. It was taken in the spring of 1970 when college students opposing the Vietnam War were shot and killed at Kent State.

When the public was told the war was winding down and President Nixon launched a new military escalation into Cambodia, the President ignited a firestorm on American campuses.

The country had been lulled into believing the "war was winding down" so the shocking escalation of the Vietnam War into Cambodia quickly brought American campuses back to the boil. On April 30, 1970, students across the United States launched a massive protest against the U.S. invasion of Cambodia. Kent State was one of hundreds of colleges that held demonstrations against the Cambodia escalation that spring.

Ohio Governor James Rhodes responded by calling the Kent State students un-American. Pounding the table in protest of the student protesters, he described them as "the worst type of people we harbor in America." In a press conference, the governor promised to drive every antiwar activist out of Kent State and eradicate "the problem." He then called up the National Guard who forced the students back into their dorms with an 11:00 p.m. curfew. When the Kent State antiwar rally was banned by the National Guard, two thousand students showed up anyway, defying their order to disperse. Tear gas canisters thrown at the crowd were thrown back. As tensions mounted, National Guard troops advanced with fixed bayonets. Some of the guardsmen knelt and aimed their weapons, but no one fired. Like a spring coil wound up tight, Sergeant Myron Pryor broke the stand-off by firing his .45 pistol, triggering a storm of bullets from the aimed rifles. Twenty-nine of the seventy-seven guardsmen fired a total of sixty-seven rounds of ammunition, killing four students and wounding nine. Two of the four students—Allison Krause and Jeffrey Miller—participated in the protest. The other two—

Sandra Scheuer and William Knox Schroeder—were walking from one class to another when they were shot dead. The average distance of the four killed students to the guardsmen was 345 feet. Some guardsmen testified they feared for their lives, but the press doubted that, given the vast distance between the students and the guard. Time Magazine concluded that "triggers were not pulled accidentally at Kent State."

The President's Commission on Campus Unrest never answered the question of how students were murdered at Kent State but concluded that "the indiscriminate firing of rifles into a crowd of students and the deaths that followed were unnecessary, unwarranted, and inexcusable."

Hearing the shocking news, songwriter Neil Young went to the woods where he composed an anthem for the American protest movement. Crosby, Stills & Nash recorded his song, and "Ohio" was soon playing on radio stations nationwide.

> "Tin soldiers and Nixon coming,
> We're finally on our own.
> This summer I hear the drumming
> Four dead in Ohio."
>
> — Neil Young

The government's invasion of Cambodia followed by four students shot and killed by National Guard troops ignited a nationwide college revolt. When another student at Jackson State College and a high school student were killed by Mississippi state troopers as well, the Chicago Seven called for a nationwide student strike. No movement leadership was necessary to get university, college, and high school students to strike, however. Five million American students stopped going to classes on their own.

Reflection Pool Protest May, 1970

David Fenton Photo

If you are a Millennial in college today, the chances are your own school went on strike and closed down too. Check it out. See if you can imagine the same spirit erupting where you go to college today.

Some students in 1970 turned their anger toward the Reserve Officers' Training Corp (ROTC) on their campus. National Guard units were mobilized in sixteen additional states and while those protests were tense, they remained mostly nonviolent. Students at New York University rolled out a giant banner that captured the mood of the campus—"They can't kill us all."

Credit and appreciation are given to Dr. George Katsiaficas who conducted extensive research for the Wentworth Institution of Boston about the spring student strike of 1970. His findings, summarized below, indicate the extraordinary scope of our protest that spring and summer. Take a moment to take this in as you realize this largely forgotten history about the Sixties movement actually happened in the United States of America. What happened before can also happen again.

Read and Reflect

The U.S. Aftermath of America's Student Strike

- Over 900 colleges and universities were closed by the end of May.
- 80% of U.S. colleges and universities held protestors with 175,000 faculty members joining in.
- Over 35,000 national guardsmen were called up.
- 30 ROTC buildings were burned or bombed.
- Highways, expressways, city streets and railroad tracks were barricaded across the country.
- Over 100,000 protests converged on Washington, D.C. while another 150,000 assembled in San Francisco.
- President Nixon, Henry Kissinger and key government officials were restricted to the White House under the protection of armed military guards with machine guns.

The White House was surrounded by a cordon of bumper-to-bumper buses.

- *Business Week* described the situation as threatening "the whole economic and social structure of the nation."
- President Nixon's memoir said the days after Kent State were "among the darkest" days of his presidency.
- Supreme Court Justice Earl Warren said that Kent State sparked the worst American crisis since the Civil War.
- 100 art museums and galleries closed in solidarity with the student strike.
- The *Wall Street Journal* reported more than 500 US GIs deserted every day in May, 1970.
- Entire companies of US troops stationed in Vietnam refused orders to invade Cambodia.
- Thousands of US soldiers wore black armbands and refused to continue fighting in Vietnam in solidarity with US students.
- Vietnam Veterans Against the War increased their membership by 50% in one month.
- Armed Forces Day resulted in marches, rallies and rock festivals at 22 US military bases involving 43 different anti-war veterans' groups.
- Military leaders cancelled Armed Forces Day events at 29 bases due to planned anti-war demonstrations.
- Nixon's chief aide, H.R. Haldeman, said "Kent State marked the beginning of Nixon's downhill slide toward Watergate."
- The first gay pride week was launched in New York on June 22, 1970 and the Gay Liberation Front sponsored their first national conference in San Francisco in August 1970.
- Feminists and the women's movement blossomed in the summer of 1970.
- US troops were withdrawn from Cambodia two months after the four students were shot at Kent State. (36)

The largest student strike in American history was massive. Many students flooded into Washington, D.C. causing president Nixon's chief speechwriter to describe Washington, D.C. as an armed camp and calling our movement the new civil war. The divide between protesters and government was deeper than the chasm of the Grand Canyon. On the one side, the President declared the youth of America were pawns of foreign communists while on the other side, the youth of America declared the Declaration of Independence would now be defended.

With thousands of protesters descending on the nation's government, the President decided to connect with the students on strike. As described by historian Stanley Karnow in his book *Vietnam: A History,* Nixon actually visited the steps of the Lincoln Memorial at 4:15 a.m. to "discuss" the war with thirty students who were conducting an all-night vigil. According to Karnow's account, Nixon treated the students to "a clumsy and condescending monologue, which he made public in an awkward attempt to display his benevolence."[35] The President's late night encounter with college students was symptomatic of the two world views of the time. The movement viewed itself as the voice of humanity. The President viewed himself as an anti-communist patriot representing the "Silent Majority."

Determined that the U.S. would never lose a war on his watch, the President declared it was his duty to destroy his enemies. Does this sound familiar when you listen to the news from today's White House? As the Watergate scandal would later reveal, the President was willing to employ illegal procedures to gather information on antiwar leaders, including every presidential candidate in the Democratic Party.

According to taped conversations in the Oval Office, Nixon's personal prejudices seemed to also include the Jewish race.

NIXON: Aren't the Chicago Seven all Jews? (Rennie) Davis is a Jew, you know.

HALDEMAN: I don't think Davis is.

NIXON: Hoffman, Hoffman's a Jew.

HALDEMAN: Abbie Hoffman is and that's so.[36]

---

35 Dr. George Katsiaficas of the Wentworth Institute, Boston. He was a leading expert on the Kent State massacre and the national student strike of May 1970. This summary of key facts is based on his extensive research and findings.
36 White House tapes.

With the war expanding and public opinion about the war unimportant to the White House, the Sixties movement did not abandon its nonviolent principles, but students did start to wonder what more they could do.

The United States would not honor elections in Vietnam because 80 percent of the Vietnamese people supported Ho Chi Minh. The Republican Party would never go down in history for losing a war to a country half the size of Texas because the United States was the leader of the "free world." The Republican government had to contain communist China by controlling the government of South Vietnam. Failure to prevent every Southeast Asian country from falling like dominos into Communist hands was not an option. The fact that every U.S. assumption about Vietnam proved inaccurate by subsequent events—that no dominos went falling after the U.S. left Vietnam and a divided Vietnam did unite to become a trading partner with the United States decades later—could not be imagined by the architects of America's war strategy.

While the Provisional Revolution Government of South Vietnam and the Democratic Republic of North Vietnam did receive military support from the Soviet Union and China during the war, events subsequently showed that Vietnam was not a puppet of those countries either. Even when the American assumptions for the war in Vietnam had been utterly refuted and the vast majority of the American public had turned against the war, the White House could never concede its policies might be wrong or misguided.

After the student strike, I returned to the Virginia farm to reflect on reports coming from European and North Vietnamese scientists who were sounding the alarm.

Genetic mutations—the result of the toxic defoliating chemical Agent Orange sprayed over the jungles of Vietnam—were showing up in Vietnamese civilians. No one could say with certainty what the long-term consequences would be but the trends were alarming. Today, we know what happened. Third and fourth generation Vietnamese are born deformed as a result of chemical Agent Orange sprayed over South Vietnam half a century ago. Agent Orange was used during the Vietnam War to clear trees, shrubs, jungles, and food crops in South Vietnam. The toxic chemical employed a mixture of two deadly herbicides,

2,4-D and 2,4,5-T. Twelve percent of South Vietnam was sprayed with the toxins. While chemical Agent Orange degrades over time, its human and environmental effects persist. Vietnam's pre-war lush forests and jungles took hundreds of years to achieve their balanced mixture of flora and fauna. In parts of South Vietnam, land erosion and landslides have decreased the soil's nutrient levels, allowing invasive grasses to take over.

Dioxin attaches itself to soil particles, which are carried by water into ponds and lakes. Vietnamese eat dioxin-contaminated fish or fowl and get sick today. Some even die...today. In the summer of 1970, many scientists correctly forecasted that dioxin consumption could change a person's internal cellular and chemical balance, creating severe health challenges, genetic mutations, or even death. And now we know that's exactly what happened.

The U.S. Agent Orange campaign called "Operation Ranch Hand" relied on an engineered chemical that could defoliate forested land and deprive guerillas of food and cover. It forced the urbanization of thousands of peasants into U.S.-dominated cities. Carried out by U.S. helicopters and low-flying C-123 Provider aircraft equipped with sprayers, pump systems, and 1,000-gallon chemical tanks, the spraying from the sky was further supported from trucks, boats, and backpack sprayers. U.S.[37] Air Force records show that 6,542 spraying missions occurred over the course of Operation Ranch Hand with ten million hectares destroyed using chemical concentrations hundreds of times greater than EPA safety standards. Five million acres of upland and mangrove forests and millions of acres of crops were ruined. Over 20 percent of South Vietnam's forests were sprayed. United Nations resolutions were drafted, declaring the U.S. violated the 1925 Geneva Protocol, regulating the use of chemical and biological weapons.

The United States claimed its use of Agent Orange was not a chemical or biological weapon but an herbicide and defoliant for depriving the enemy of cover. American GIs were never told how dangerous it was or what the protocols were for keeping the chemicals sealed. When the war ended, many American GIs came home poisoned while the dioxins that settled into the soil and sediment of Vietnam entered the food chain through animals and fish that are still consumed today.

---

37 Karnow, Stanley. *Vietnam: A History*. New York: Penguin, 1997.

The use of chemical substances toxic to plants is prohibited by international law. The Vietnamese Government has repeatedly stated more than three million Vietnamese directly suffered from chemical Agent Orange. Counting the disabled in Laos, Cambodia and the United States, the number Agent Orange afflicted may be closer to five million people. Nevertheless, the U.S. has remained adamant even today that every scientific or government study on this subject is unreliable and any settlement with Vietnamese victims is out of the question. Even when the Red Cross lowered the victim estimates to one million people, government admission that the United States should have liability for what happened has been steadfastly avoided.

In recent years, I have met Vietnamese who suffer from genetic mutations from chemical Agent Orange. While it is hard to accept that genetic deformities are appearing in newborn babies today from Agent Orange sprayed decades ago, the year this book was published, 300,000 4th generation Vietnamese were born deformed.

That was my concern when I was thinking about our next steps following the student strike and that remains my concern today. Since we have the technologies today to clean up the soil in Vietnam and return the quality of life to most victims of Agent Orange, healing the wounds of war and supporting the victims of Agent Orange could be one of the early campaigns for today's movement to change the world. Since we have the know-how to clean up radiation poisoning in Chernobyl and lead poisoning in Flint, what a joy it would be to get started.

In the summer of 1970, the poisoning of people, water, and soil in Vietnam meant our next step as a movement had to be stronger. It was not time for the antiwar movement to cool down. It was time to fire up.

I thought about the times when civil disobedience had been promoted by Mahatma Gandhi. I thought about the civil rights civil disobedience in Birmingham promoted by Dr. Martin Luther King, Jr. I asked myself, what would Gandhi and King do now?

If The Government Will Not Stop The War in Vietnam We Will Stop the Government of the United States

Chapter 7

CIVIL DISOBEDIENCE

Our Decision to Shut Down the Government

When students went back to their classes in the fall of 1970, the wind beneath our wings was spent and our passion seemed to have faded away. When an antiwar meeting was called on campus, only the most committed organizers showed up. The movement was gone.

The February 22, 1971 *Time Magazine* issue described our mood in a cover story, "The Cooling of America." Everyone felt the chill in the air. When I proposed large-scale, non-violent civil disobedience in Washington, D.C. to a gathering of the National Mobilization Committee Against the War in Vietnam, I was met with a stony silence. Our coalition had no issue with civil disobedience, but no one believed it could be done.

I felt it possible and wanted to test the waters. One evening, looking out of my Washington apartment window, I saw my hippie neighbors across the street and a wild-haired idea came to me. Since I did not have the support of our coalition for civil disobedience, perhaps my neighbors could help me set up a temporary office and answer phones while I toured a few colleges to float the idea. When I pitched my proposal to them, they were excited. They agreed to manage a D.C. office while I went on the road. When a supporter contributed to our budget, I was off and running to see for myself whether large-scale civil disobedience was possible.

My first stop was Brown University. Local campus activists met me at the airport and said there would be little response from their student body. But when five thousand students packed the auditorium, I spoke for an hour about chemical Agent Orange in Vietnam. I could hear a pin drop. When I ended by saying, "If the Government of the United States will not stop the war in Vietnam, then we will stop the Government of the United

States," the hushed room transformed into a deafening roar. As the students stood and cheered, I knew then and there a new chapter could be written for our movement and our country.

For my part in America's largest civil disobedience arrest in history, I got to see a large and complex mobilization take shape. Once our coalition saw it coming too, their support returned and everyone pitched in. I didn't close my neighbors' hippie office either but let it morph into the "MayDay tribe" that basically organized the direct action component that shook the government of the United States to its core.

Throughout the fall into the New Year, I watched our support for large-scale civil disobedience grow every day until it did become the most complex U.S. anti-war mobilization ever attempted.

Consisting of three interrelated events spanning a period of two weeks, the direct action plan included: 1) a broad-based anti-war rally in Washington, D.C. where participants could expect not to be arrested, 2) one week of anti-war protests from Vietnam veterans who would return their medals and awards won in Vietnam back to Congress, and 3) a culminating rally for people supporting the nonviolent civil disobedience mobilization during Monday morning rush hour traffic.

Our plan was complex but straightforward: to bring the public's anti-war voice back into focus and stop the Government from conducting its war business while the whole world was watching.

When a government becomes unresponsive to its voting majority and war crimes are committed in the name of the people, is civil disobedience appropriate? How do we know when direct action is patriotic or an unpatriotic affront to the values of a democracy? From the American Revolution to the Sixties Revolution, the United States debated the question. Does patriotism mean every citizen must support its government when it commits crimes against humanity? The question facing today's movement is similar: does patriotism mean we have to normalize White House fake news and live with the dismantling of our institutions and values or does patriotism call for massive, nonviolent civil disobedience that shakes the government to its core? When does the media, civil service, opposition party and the majority of the American electorate fundamentally resist? Do we resist a gridlock government when every ecosystem on Earth is under assault and civilization's unsustainable practices threaten the life of the planet?

The Sixties came to a juncture when we had to face some difficult questions. Our choice was to (1) accept the patriotism of "my country right or wrong," or (2) publicly challenge our own government for war crimes. Today's choice may be even more ominous: (1) blindly set the table for humanity's last supper or (2) rise to the occasion and change the world.

Here is a Sixties story that seems relevant again. Today's movement will be wise to take this in and consider its meaning.

In 1971, our movement abandoned the historic patriotism of my country right or wrong to embrace a new patriotism that could bring international attention to America's war crimes and challenge the nonresponsive nature of government itself.

When Mahatma Gandhi prepared for India's pivotal Salt March, he followed a strategy of announcing to the public the details of his plan. He let the whole world know the times, places, and tactics of his civil disobedience intentions. Gandhi's movement embraced complete transparency. But the British were still caught flat-footed and unprepared. I decided to follow that strategy as well. We published a Mayday tactical manual that pinpointed the exact locations of every Washington site we planned to close with civil disobedience. We announced our plan in advance so the government and the media knew what part of Washington we were going to block. We also announced that we intended to create the largest arrest in American history.

The New Patriotism

David Fenton Photo

After the demonstrations in Chicago, the media was fixated on the question of permits. For this demonstration in Washington, D.C., they wanted to know whether the federal government would issue permits for our civil disobedience or "repeat the mistakes of Chicago." Because a police riot had resulted when Chicago permits were denied, President Nixon decided he had to grant us permits.

I wasn't confident our permits would hold by with permits in hand, our team began preparing for our three-stage mobilization.

- **Stage 1** would begin in front of the Capitol building with an event that would mirror our traditional nonviolent mass rallies of the past. Our estimates ranged from 150,000 to 250,000 people.
- **Stage 2** would be a smaller demonstration but a first in American history. American veterans who fought in Vietnam would return their medals of honor back to Congress.
- **Stage 3** would be 100,000 people sitting in roads and on bridges during Monday morning rush hour traffic to stop the government from continuing the war.

Since I was the coordinator of "peace coffeehouses" at ten U.S. military bases and often spoke with active duty GIs who came to our coffeehouses, I knew our antiwar movement was popular with many soldiers. We had considerable support among American GIs heading for Vietnam. During one of my visits to Fort Bragg, I was accompanied by Jane Fonda.

It amazes me that half a century after the Vietnam War there are people who are still upset with Jane Fonda for her fact-finding trip to Vietnam. When she was in North Vietnam, she was photographed next to Vietnamese resistance fighters and the picture went out to the world, inflaming some American "patriots."

When Jane Fonda accompanied me to Fort Bragg, it was just the two of us going onto a large base together. Thousands of GIs surrounded us as word spread like wildfire that she was on their base. Jane spoke her convictions too, saying what most Americans would agree with today. While the audience included many antiwar GI friends, not every soldier was ready to embrace her new type of patriotism that day— that Americans can support their GIs by bringing them home. People who say they "hate" Jane Fonda for "not supporting our GIs" may not realize she was describing scientifically documented U.S. war crimes in Southeast Asia like burning down villages and killing women and children. She believed these U.S. war crimes were not patriotic at all. Should you ever have the opportunity to talk with Jane yourself, please take the opportunity to thank her. History has shown she was right that the U.S. Government was the misguided party about the Vietnam War. For her courage and patriotism, you can thank her now.

American GIs Against the War in 1971

David Fenton Photo

In Washington, D.C., active duty GIs and Vietnam War veterans abandoned the American tradition of "my country, right or wrong" in an unprecedented about face. With their Purple Hearts, Bronze Stars, and other distintinguished military honors, they carried the banner of Jane Fonda's new patriotism to the steps of the U.S. Congress where they returned their military medals back to Congress as they embraced a patriotism never previously witnessed from U.S. servicemen.

John Kerry, a Navy lieutenant, had just returned from Vietnam and also came to this event in Washington. He was an unknown person who had the courage to advance the new patriotism himself. It also launched his new public persona. After graduating from Yale University in 1966, he joined the U.S. Navy where he won the Silver Star, the Bronze Star, and three Purple Hearts in Vietnam. He was a war hero who returned from battle having witnessed unspeakable atrocities and had the courage to join thousands of other Vietnam Veterans against the war. On April 22, 1971, he was twenty seven years old when he appeared before the Senate Foreign Relations wearing his ribbons on a rumpled fatigue shirt as NBC News broadcast his testimony to the nation.

John Kerry was a returning Vietnam War hero who refused to stay silent. His patriotism called him to reject the U.S. government's war crimes in Vietnam.

"Thirty years from now," Kerry said, "when our brothers go down the street without a leg, without an arm or a face, and small boys ask why, we will be able to say 'Vietnam'

and not mean a desert, not a filthy, obscene memory but mean instead the place where America finally turned and where soldiers like us helped it in the turning."[38]

John Kerry recalled for the senators a gathering several months earlier where highly decorated veterans—over 150 honorably discharged men—testified in Detroit about U.S. war crimes in Vietnam that were committed with the full understanding of their officers. Kerry described the emotional atmosphere as these servicemen relived the nightmare of what the United States made them do. In bringing these stories to public light, he spoke to an American public that longed to end a misguided war. Donning the mantle of the new patriotism, he delivered this message to the senators:

> The veterans in Detroit told stories that at times they had personally raped, cut off ears, cut off heads, taped wires from portable telephones to human genitals and turned up the power, cut off limbs, blew up bodies, randomly shot at civilians, razed villages in a fashion reminiscent of Genghis Khan, shot cattle and dogs for fun, poisoned food stocks, and generally ravaged the countryside of South Vietnam in addition to the normal ravage of war and the normal and very

38 Information about air and truck support for Agent Orange defoliation in South Vietnam was largely provided by Wikipedia, File:US-troops-spray-Agent-Orange-from-river boatVietnam.ogv http://en.wikipedia.org/wiki/File:North_Vietnamese_Antiaircraft_Weapons.jpg

particular ravaging which is done by the applied bombing power of this country.

We who have come here to Washington could be quiet. We could hold our silence. We could not tell what went on in Vietnam but we feel because of what threatens this country—not the reds but the crimes which we are committing that threaten it—that we have to speak out...

In our opinion and from our experience, there is nothing in South Vietnam which could happen that realistically threatens the United States of America. And to attempt to justify the loss of one American life in Vietnam, Cambodia or Laos by linking such loss to the preservation of freedom...is to us the height of criminal hypocrisy and it is that kind of hypocrisy which we feel has torn this country apart.

Each day to facilitate the process by which the United States washes her hands of Vietnam someone has to give up his life so that the United States doesn't have to admit something that the entire world already knows, so that we can't say that we have made a mistake. Someone has to die so that President Nixon won't be, and these are his words, "the first President to lose a war."

How do you ask a man to be the last man to die for a mistake? We are here in Washington to say that the problem of this war is not just a question of war and diplomacy. It is part and parcel of everything that we are trying as human beings to communicate to people in this country—the question of racism which is rampant in the military and so many other questions such as the use of weapons; the hypocrisy in our taking umbrage at the Geneva Conventions and using that as justification for a continuation of this war when we are more guilty than any other body of violations of those Geneva Conventions; in the use of free fire zones, harassment interdiction fire, search and destroy missions, the bombings, the torture of prisoners, all accepted policy by many units in South Vietnam. That is what we are trying to say. It is part

> and parcel of everything. We wish that a merciful God could wipe away our own memories of that service as easily as this administration has wiped away their memories of us.[39]

Following these Senate hearings, Vietnam veterans launched an extraordinary American protest they called "a limited incursion into the country of Congress." With awe-inspiring courage and patriotism, American veterans from every branch of the military stated their names, units, and citations before throwing their medals, awards, ribbons, discharge papers, and war mementos onto the steps of the U.S. Capitol. For three hours, one by one, they tossed their decorations of bravery back to the U.S. government. One veteran said, "I hope someday I can return to Vietnam and help rebuild the country we tore apart." Another announced, "Here are my merit badges for murder." Paul Winter took the microphone to pray for forgiveness as he threw back his Silver Star, Bronze Star, and Distinguished Service Cross before limping away.[40]

Fifty veterans then marched to the Pentagon and turned themselves in as war criminals. Perplexed and confused, Pentagon officials wrote down their names before sending them away. Other veterans planted trees on the Mall as a declaration of life. Some conducted services for their wounded warriors at the Walter Reed Army Medical Center. Led by mothers of soldiers killed in Vietnam, another 1,100 veterans marched across the Lincoln Memorial Bridge to the Arlington Cemetery for a memorial service beneath the Tomb of the Unknown Soldier. As they approached the cemetery, the government locked the gate, forcing mothers of sons killed in Vietnam to place their wreaths for their loved ones outside the gate. As the march continued toward the Capitol, U.S. Senators and Representatives joined in, including McCloskey, Abzug, Edwards, Chisholm, Muskie and Rein, who never to the memo that opposing an unjust war was unpatriotic.

As these elected representatives spoke to the veteran assembly with a passionate support, the Justice Department issued an injunction to stop the veterans from camping out on the Mall. The District Court of Appeals immediately lifted that injunction so the

---

39 Vietnam War veteran John Kerry's testimony before the Senate Foreign Relations Committee, April 22, 1971.

40 The Veteran. "Vets' History: Operation Dewey Canyon II." April 1977. http://www.vvaw.org/veteran/article/?id=1656.

veterans could camp out anyway. Chief Justice Warren Burger, however, quickly reissued it again, establishing a new judicial record for the speediest reversal of a reversal in court history. In other words, there were two types of patriots in Washington, D.C. Special White House Counsel Charles Colson was one type, demanding that more had to be done to undermine the organizers of this veterans' event and insisting that the federal government must find ways to show that Vietnam Veterans Against the War was "a fringe group" financed from "questionable sources that did not represent real veterans." The second type were veterans who rejected the government's premise that the United States had gone to Vietnam to "win the hearts and minds of the people." Putting their new patriotism on full public display, they openly supported Vietnamese orphans. Some adopted crippled Vietnamese children. They were veterans who decide to stop waving their flags to tell the truth.

Vietnam veterans came to Washington knowing they could face arrest for camping out and were prepared for tear gas and arrests. When they were reassured by the park police they would not be arrested despite orders from the highest court to incarcerate them all, a Washington newspaper headline read, "Vets Overrule the Supreme Court."

In 1932, World War I veterans camped out in Washington, demanding their service bonuses. President Hoover sent in troops and used tear gas, bullets, bayonets, and torches to destroy the veterans' camp before driving them out of the city. In 1971, the Vietnam Veterans Against the War came to Washington again but this time they touched the heart of America with their new patriotism.

Movements that generate enormous public support force politicians to have second thoughts. Nixon could only respond to the new patriotism of these American veterans by publicly declaring "I see no reason to go in and arrest the veterans and put them into jail at this time."

Following the Vietnam veterans' stunning and inspiring second stage, the third stage began—the largest civil disobedience arrest in America.

This final stage began with a rally for all the people who were ready to face arrest. As we gathered on the Mall, we were one hundred thousand people in Washington, D.C. The Beach Boys performed on stage. When I walked up to the mic to speak, I was speechless seeing this sea of human courage and realizing the immense power of ordinary people when they unite to defend the American dream.

That night, the demonstrators "slept" in churches that had become our regional centers for people willing to go to jail. Nearly 35,000 activists camped out in West Potomac Park as well. Imagine, if you can, the sight of a massive tent city in the center of Washington, D.C. It made me realize the enormity of who we were and the significance of what was about to happen.

On a Saturday May night, the warm beautiful evening was perfect for a magical festival of life. I was pleased our permit to camp out was honored, but was not surprised when the White House abandoned the permit the following evening.

Sunday night before our Monday direct action in rush hour traffic, Park and Washington Metropolitan Police suited up in riot gear and raided our tent city, charging our "shining city on the hill" and knocking down thousands of tents while hurling tear gas into the fleeing crowd. Tens of thousands of campers flooded the D.C. Reflecting Pool and the Lincoln Memorial area. Many of the displaced campers moved into their own cars or regrouped at one of our designated churches or college dorms. The police raid did cause Sunday evening traffic gridlock, but not at the time we had stated in our plan.

The people who came to Washington for civil disobedience came from many geographical regions. Each region took responsibility for one of the twenty-one Monday morning sit-in sites located at circles, bridges, and highway intersections. Our plan was laid out in our May Day tactical manual that described each of the sites we would nonviolently block. Making it publicly known that our goal was to confront the government's intransigence about the Vietnam war, we told every government employee and every elected official that we intended to impede their rush hour morning traffic and close their government down.

Arriving for Mayday
David Fenton Photo

Arrested for MayDay

Prison for Mayday

The Boston region and other regions sent representatives to study their sites months before the sit-in occurred and hundreds of other organizers devoted themselves to the many preparation tasks as well.

This is the story of what happened during America's largest civil disobedience in history.

I don't want to begin by leaving the impression that our movement was masterful in its logistics or good at its rush-hour traffic timing. The fact is our adrenaline-laced excitement kept everyone up all night before the morning event. By 5:30 a.m. Monday, patience was thrown to the wind as thousands of demonstrators headed out to their regional sites hours before the Monday morning traffic began. My entire team joined me in one loud "Oops," as we watched our protest timing implode. In our defense, we were in our 20s and frankly it was hard to sleep Sunday night when the government was deploying thousands of police and military units into the city. President Nixon called in the U.S. Marines, who landed on the Mall. With police in place and demonstrations out and about before sunrise, it was easy for demonstrators to be driven out of the city by police pincer actions without being arrested.

The government's plan was based on preparations it had created in the 1960s to combat urban disorders. The movement's plan was based on understandings of historic traffic patterns. Our plan was to arrive at each designated site by 7:00 a.m. That plan fell apart when 10,000 federal troops were deployed into the city throughout the night. Everyone was excited as U.S. Army soldiers and Marines moved into D.C. from bases up and down the East Coast. Troop transports were landing at nearby Andrews Air Force Base every three minutes, including 4,000 paratroopers from the U.S. 82nd Airborne Division that reinforced the 5,100 D.C. Metropolitan Police and 2,000 D.C. National Guardsmen as needed. Every national monument, federal park, and traffic circle deployed troops to protect their perimeters.

Who could sleep when thousands of paratroopers and U.S. Marines were descending by helicopter onto the grounds of the Washington Monument?

By 8:00 a.m. Monday, the troops and police had largely secured our twenty-one bridges and intersections. Massive sweeps of the area using canisters of tear gas targeted anyone in our designated sites. A group of hardhat construction workers came out to show their support for Nixon's "law and order" and they were arrested too. After the first 7,000 demonstrators were detained, city prisons reached their carrying capacity so an emergency detention center next to RFK Stadium with an eight-foot high fence became the government's fallback prison for thousands more who were arrested. Since the government's makeshift "prison" had no food, water, or sanitary facilities, nearby residents graciously brought in supplies for us from their homes. Our protests continued throughout the day and into Monday night, but the police dispersed any crowd, however small, that tried to gather. Police helicopters lobbed tear gas anywhere protesters assembled, including Georgetown University's lower athletic field where protesters were camping. They also used a new type of gas that induced vomiting.

Abbie Hoffman for MayDay

David Fenton Photo

President Nixon had left Washington for his Western White House in California, but he remained in constant communication with his White House staff. He was adamant that no federal worker except himself should leave the city or take the day off. Every civil servant had to navigate through the demonstrators and the massive police lines around our sit-in sites because the government was not going to be closed or intimidated by any "rag-tag youth movement." With police sweeps and indiscriminate arrests going on at the crack of dawn Monday morning, many federal commuters were seriously delayed getting to work, but eventually did get to their offices. Despite Nixon's orders to federal employees to go to work, I appreciated the courage of the Federal Employees for Peace who got a permit and held a rally at Lafayette Park in front of the White House to protest the war.

President Nixon and his advisers responded to our public call for civil disobedience by sending undercover agents into our organizations. They did their best to follow us while securing the transmission frequencies of our "walkie-talkies" to monitor our conversations. The White House set up a basement command post for command and control. Their initial plan to delegate security to the Washington police quickly shifted as the direct action time grew closer. While most demonstrators remained nonviolent, some did push trashcans, parked cars, and tree limbs into the streets. Martial law was never officially declared, but it was certainly in effect.

When our civil disobedience was over, the press proclaimed our movement had "failed." According to the media, we delayed the government, but did not shut it down. While we should never be remembered for our logistical brilliance, the White House was shaken. In fact, history has shown that MayDay did change an entrenched Oval Office.

Because of our poor logistics, the nation's pinnacle civil disobedience event caused far fewer arrests than we planned. The authorities arrested a total of 12,614 people, and Abbie Hoffman and I were among them.

As Abbie and I were escorted into the Justice Department surrounded by thirty federal agents, their demeanor gave new meaning to the term "rigid adult." Sober, serious and stern, they escorted us down a dimly-lit corridor to a processing center. I was in front of this solemn suit parade while Abbie—joking, laughing and having a great time as usual—was right behind me. I will never forget what happened that day. Any idea that these agents would smile—much less laugh out loud—was inconceivable given their somber mood but Abbie couldn't help himself. He began to poke fun at himself. Then he made fun of me. "We are so pathetic," he said, with a whining poor-me tone. "Caught red handed for our terrible behavior, oh no, we did it. Take me to where I need to go to confess my crimes. I'm guilty. He's guilty too. We both did it." His humor was infectious and I started smiling. But the miracle of miracles was seeing grins appear on the arresting agents. Abbie turned their grins into smiles until a few of the Suits started to chuckle. Soon everyone was laughing out loud inside this law-and-order fortress of the U.S. Justice Department.

That day I felt honored to witness the power of humor to cut through a tension thicker than molasses. All by himself, Abbie Hoffman transformed thirty federal agents who want to put us in prison and throw away the key.

Abbie and I were now facing round two of the Chicago 7 trial. While it seemed exciting to us at the time, the Justice Department quickly figured it out. They evaluated the consequences of inflicting themselves with another migraine headache public trial, and our prospect of twenty years in prison was quietly dropped. Thousands of others who came to Washington and were arrested were suddenly free to go as well. That didn't mean the view of us in the White House changed but it did suggest our impact was consequential.

As I researched this event for this book I ran across some recorded Oval Office conversations, representing a "tradition" that was started by President Eisenhower and emulated by Kennedy, Johnson, and Nixon. Believing that recording a meeting meant historical accuracy was secured and people who met with the president were "on the record," President Nixon recorded more than 3,700 hours of his own conversations from February 16, 1971 to July 12, 1973. Microphones were installed in the Oval Office, the Cabinet Room, and Camp David as well as on telephones in the Oval Office. Reading the transcripts of the Nixon White House conversations during this time helped me better understand the thinking of the White House about us. These recorded conversations made it plain that our movement had one vision for America while the Oval Office another. These slightly edited transcripts speak volumes about the thinking in the White House during this time of upheaval and resistance. There is not much written in history books about this extraordinary event. Millennials readying this account may think it has to be

Rennie's science fiction—but it's not. These conversations inside the Oval Office actually happened.

Imagine our glee when we get to hear the transcripts of Donald J. Trump speaking 'privately' inside today's White House.

President Nixon's perspective about our civil disobedience is part of the presidential archive available to the public. Nixon's own comments about us before and after the May Day event were recorded in Oval Office conversations.

NIXON: They arrest people that obstruct traffic, don't they?

EHRLICHMAN: That's right. That's right.

NIXON: Good.

EHRLICHMAN: And they get off with a ten dollar fine or something of that kind. Now if there's violence or anything of that sort, then you respond.

NIXON: Yeah.

EHRLICHMAN: And the chances are that the Congress would respond at that point with a stiffer law.

NIXON: Well, let me say this. There's no damn congressman or senator going to vote against it.

EHRLICHMAN: That's right.

NIXON: Except [Senator] Birch Bayh [D-Indiana], maybe.

EHRLICHMAN: Well, you see, these fellows will get off with a misdemeanor. It's anywhere from ten to twenty-five dollars for obstructing traffic.

NIXON: Yeah.

EHRLICHMAN: And that's not much of a deterrent. Matter of fact, their directions to their protesters say that they should not post bail and that they should try and clog up the jail facilities.

NIXON: That's great.

EHRLICHMAN: So this gets to be a little contest as to how many jails we can find within fifty miles, you know.

NIXON: We'll find them.

EHRLICHMAN: But we can find plenty of them. And my feeling is that [Washington police chief] Jerry Wilson ought to be told that this is a police problem, we have a lot of confidence in him, and that we just—

NIXON: Right. Exactly. And that we'll back him up.

EHRLICHMAN: Sure, and that he would handle this as he would handle any Similar difficulty.

NIXON: Right. Yeah, but let's face it; it isn't as bad as Berkeley has had or San Francisco has had, yet.

EHRLICHMAN: I think that you can expect that these people will be in very massive numbers and that probably this police department will be swamped. They will not be able to handle the numbers.

NIXON: What do you mean "massive numbers"?

EHRLICHMAN: Oh, I think—

NIXON: A thousand?

EHRLICHMAN: In any one of these twenty intersections, you'll have anywhere from 700 to 1,000, 1,500, something of that kind.

NIXON: Who's organizing them?

EHRLICHMAN: It's a highly structured operation, and it's quite beautifully organized actually by Rennie Davis and a whole group of more or less professional organizers that have been at this for a long time.

NIXON: Why did [Senator Hubert H.] Humphrey take what had seemed to me a rather soft line in trying to clear the [Senate] galleries then if it was Rennie Davis and that group?

EHRLICHMAN: I don't know. I don't know. He later went out on the lawn and talked with them, and they made a fool of him.

NIXON: How'd they do that?

EHRLICHMAN: Well, they—

NIXON: That wasn't on television, though?

EHRLICHMAN: Yeah, it was. He was standing talking to them and some fellow came up and made a "V" sign over his head, and he looked like a rabbit, you know.

NIXON: Yeah.

EHRLICHMAN: And they continued to do that and they were all laughing at him behind him and, of course, he couldn't see it while he was playing to the camera.

EHRLICHMAN: The question in my mind is whether you can afford to be away on Monday, because that's the first day of the obstructions, when they plan to block the bridges and so forth.

NIXON: Think I should come back?

EHRLICHMAN: I'm inclined to think you should. I think you should be here, and that seemed to be the consensus at the meeting just now.

NIXON: I'm all for it. Well, could I come back—

EHRLICHMAN: Sunday night, something of that—early Monday morning, maybe?

NIXON: But I don't have to be here all day Monday, do I?

EHRLICHMAN: The blockage would be from 7:00 a.m. until noon. And—

NIXON: Then I should come back Sunday night?

EHRLICHMAN: Well, I think if you were simply to announce your itinerary about now so that it was obvious that you were planning to come back Monday all the time.

NIXON: Right.

EHRLICHMAN: Then it wouldn't matter too much what time you got in on Monday.

NIXON: Yeah. I'll be back Monday, right. I'd like to have a couple of days off in California Saturday and Sunday.

EHRLICHMAN: Sure. Sure. But I think if you—

NIXON: And then get on the plane Monday morning—

EHRLICHMAN: Right.

NIXON: —and get back here, and get back about three or four in the afternoon—

EHRLICHMAN: And by the time you get here, why the thing will have had its first spasm.

NIXON: Good, I'll do it. I'll be back. I'd just as soon be back here. I like to be in the fight.

EHRLICHMAN: Well, I think symbolically, particularly if you have to go to the Congress for relief, you ought to be here.

NIXON: Good, I'm delighted. I couldn't agree more with it.

On Tuesday, following the Monday May 3 civil disobedience, president Nixon and H.R. Haldeman, White House Chief of Staff, met in the Oval Office, the "morning after" the civil disobedience.

NIXON: Wow, are they going to try again tomorrow morning? Is that the whole deal?

HALDEMAN: I don't know. They've got one judge now who has issued a show-cause on the arrests...

NIXON: Left wing [unintelligible].

HALDEMAN: —he objected to the mass arrests.

NIXON: Mitchell knows how to handle the case?

HALDEMAN: Yeah.

HALDEMAN: They picked up Rennie Davis on a specific arrest. The FBI went out and got him. Pretty good coverage on the damage and disruption. There's only one or two that have come out for the demonstrators. Muskie didn't come out very strongly against them.

NIXON: No, he would've waffled. What do you think is the country's reaction to it?

HALDEMAN: I think it's going to be that there were a lot of bad people here that were well-handled, that didn't let them tear the thing apart.

NIXON: Right.

HALDEMAN: They've got a plan for the Federal Employees for Peace to have a meeting in the Lafayette Park tomorrow at noon. Our thought is to have Justice [Department] go for an injunction, which they think they can get and turn it off. And it would seem like it's a good thing not to have happen at this point.

NIXON: How could Justice get an injunction?

HALDEMAN: I don't know. They seem to think they can just on the basis of all the problems around or something. But TV would make a big thing out of the Federal employees demonstrating against the Federal Government.

NIXON: What the hell is this? Those dirty punks! Who the hell are they? They're a bunch of goddamn State Department bastards that [unintelligible].

HALDEMAN: They're probably mostly HEW, HUD, and OEO. I would bet there won't be any State Department people there. I think they got—

NIXON: The word?

NIXON: Bunch of bastards in the bureaucracy!

HALDEMAN: In the normal course, it wouldn't make any difference. The reason for not letting them do it is that TV will make such a big thing out of—

NIXON: How will they enjoin them, on what grounds?

HALDEMAN: I don't know. They have a permit. They filed for a permit and they got it.

NIXON: Oh.

HALDEMAN: They have to move on some other grounds. But I think they are doing it on the basis of the other activity here or something.

NIXON: The little bastards will be out on something else. Yeah.

HALDEMAN: Federal Employees for Clean Air.

NIXON: Why, they're the dirtiest damn people there are! They throw crap all over the place. Ragged, unkempt, as though the ecology of my time wasn't discovered.

Later that day, Chief Counsel Charles Colson joined the President and Chief of Staff for more conversations about us:

NIXON: How are all your operations looking?

COLSON: We have six senators, possibly more, who will speak tomorrow on attacking Muskie and Humphrey by name.

HALDEMAN: Really?

COLSON: It took courage. We've sent them up speeches this morning.

NIXON: On what ground attack them?

COLSON: Well, two grounds. Muskie on his charges against the FBI for surveillance...

NIXON: Right.

COLSON: and (speaking with) Rennie Davis on Earth Day.

NIXON: Right.

COLSON: We're sure it comes back to haunt him.

NIXON: Right.

COLSON: Humphrey has endorsed them and in fact encouraged them. Muskie for his open endorsement of the April twenty-fourth demonstration for visiting demonstrators on the Mall—

NIXON: What's Kennedy doing about all of this?

COLSON: He's out of town, conveniently—

NIXON: Smart as hell.

HALDEMAN: Shit, he really is—

NIXON: He was with the veterans.

HALDEMAN: He was with the veterans and he quit them. You know, just incredible demagoguery! He put on that flight jacket with the Presidential seal on it to go down and talk to the veterans.

COLSON: He's playing it the smartest of all. He's had nothing to say about April twenty-fourth [our stage two]. And now with Vietnam Veterans Against the War, I found him yesterday in his office and he would not comment. Reporters called four times yesterday and once again this morning and still didn't get a comment. He's not going to get caught on this one.

NIXON: Now is the time for you to charge up our guys. They should take the offensive. Put these in the goddamn lily-livered mealy-mouths and stand up and kick them in the balls.

COLSON: Well, this group that caused the trouble this week was a co-sponsor of the April twenty-fourth show. Rennie Davis was—

NIXON: The social issue—kids smoking pot and raising hell—this gives a bad name to the whole demonstration.

COLSON: Yes.

NIXON: Our guys should play it in terms of their hypocrisy: they [Democratic Senators] endorsed the demonstrators. In other words, I wouldn't say they changed their minds. Let them deny it. The way to make the charge is to just charge that they endorsed demonstration and then let them deny. That's the way to do it.

COLSON: Well, if we got a little bit of law-and-order concern in the country as a result of what happened this week, it becomes a very bad time politically to attack Edgar Hoover or the FBI.

HALDEMAN: Arresting Rennie Davis—

COLSON: Yeah.

HALDEMAN: —doesn't hurt, did it?

COLSON: [Walter] Cronkite did not let people forget last night, "this is not dissimilar from Chicago."

COLSON: No.

NIXON: That's what burned them up in Chicago: a lot of them got roughed up. These police didn't rough anybody up—

COLSON: No.

NIXON: —except some of the damn bums.

NIXON: Is the position of the administration clear, that we're talking, strong and firm?

COLSON: Yes, sir.

NIXON: No doubts about that? Nobody is squealing about our position, huh?

COLSON: No, not at all.

NIXON: Then it's across the country now?

COLSON: Well, I didn't see much beyond Washington, but—

NIXON: But you think it is getting across?

COLSON: I think so, yes, sir.

NIXON: Well, let's come out for the [Washington Police] Chief... law and order.

COLSON: Well, he [Police Chief Wilson] did it beautifully.

HALDEMAN: He's sort of a George Patton-type guy—

COLSON: Yeah.

NIXON: Tries to charge up his troops.

HALDEMAN: He was out on the front lines at four o'clock yesterday morning, and covered every trouble point. He was zooming all over the city.

COLSON: In his motorcycle.

NIXON: His motorcycle?

HALDEMAN: He's like that, the old-time great generals.

NIXON: Great guy.

HALDEMAN: Well, his line yesterday showed great skill, when they said, "Well, don't you think you moved too hard and too fast on it?" And he said, "We'll let the American people be the judge of that."

NIXON: So aren't we lucky, aren't we lucky to have him?

HALDEMAN: We really are.

NIXON: That we got him rather than some dumb jerk like that jackass Murphy, who's in New York.

HALDEMAN: Got guts. Nothing bothers him. Like that last demonstration, when they were attacking the Justice Department, he went in there and personally ordered the crowd to disperse. They didn't disperse and he personally threw the first tear gas canister in.

NIXON: Good.

HALDEMAN: Damn right, he made sure he's very Patton-like. He made sure the cameras were there.

NIXON: That's the way to handle them.

HALDEMAN: With this kind of police force, you've got to have a guy like Patton.

NIXON: Half of them are Negroes.

HALDEMAN: —you got a potentially shaky police force in here that, because they keep pouring these blacks in.

NIXON: We may have to re-issue the word "law and order."

COLSON: Mr. President, it causes people to arch their backs and say, "Well, by God, we're not going to be pushed around by kids in the street." They're worried on the Hill that if they now start pressing for an immediate legislative end to the war, it'll look like they caved in to this kind of protest in the street.

NIXON: Somebody has got to take that on—these people are giving in to the protesters. The idea that policy is to be made in the Senate, it's not to be in the House, and it's not to be made in the streets. They ought to start cracking that hard, don't you think so, Bob?

HALDEMAN: Yes.

NIXON: Did you find anybody that is willing to walk up and tear down the goddamn Viet Cong flag? I want it torn down every place they have it. We can't have that flag flying around here.

Fight, get them into a fight about that! That's a lovely thing to get into a fight about. Nobody has a right to carry a damn flag of an enemy around here! Don't you agree? What do you think, Chuck?

COLSON: I agree with you.

NIXON: All right.

NIXON: Get the hardhats, or somebody—

COLSON: Well, the hardhats turned out up on Pennsylvania Avenue en masse yesterday.

NIXON: Yeah, anyone who would just up and bust the bastards.

HALDEMAN: Rather than us giving them the business, they (demonstrators) have been trying to move the hardhats to join with them—

NIXON: I know, I know, I know.

HALDEMAN: —so this is good for (the hard hats) to take them on.[41]

Here is a final conversation with the President and his administrative assistant, Rose Mary Woods, that same day should you want to understand what the President of the United States really thought about us:

NIXON: What do you think of these people that have been raising hell? Did you see any of that?

WOODS: They're awful-looking people.

NIXON: Yeah. They got the long hair and beards—out there stinking and raising hell and all on dope, you know. I'm glad that Humphrey and all the rest are tied right in with them.

WOODS: They're trying to repudiate it, but—

---

41 Taped White House Transcripts. NIXON PRESIDENTIAL Tape Subject Log [rev. 8/07 Conv. No. 491-14 (cont.) and http://whitehousetapes.net/glossary/term/159.

NIXON: Too late.

WOODS: —It's too late. They've been with them all this time.

NIXON: I really feel we got to railroad this. The networks were trying desperately to make these people look peaceful and decent. What a lousy bunch of bastards they were.

WOODS: Yeah.[42]

The largest arrest in American history was not our final antiwar mobilization, but it was our most impactful. Historians will debate whether our civil disobedience was appropriate in Washington, D.C. For today's movement that is pondering what to do when the results of an election fail to reflect the majority of voting electorate, this Sixties story may have relevance again.

In the past when direct action was used to influence public policy or change an illegitimate, racist culture, it could lead to prison terms for the protesters. Prison terms for sheriffs who brutalized demonstrators or government officials committing war crimes were rare. In America's 1971 civil disobedience, however, the historic pattern was challenged. The American Civil Liberties Union brought a class action suit representing the vast majority of the detained demonstrators, and the U.S. Congress acknowledged the illegal nature of the indiscriminate arrests. Congress agreed to pay a settlement to the people arrested, making them the first U.S citizens ever to receive compensation for having their constitutional rights of assembly violated.

President Nixon, on the other hand, became the first American president to resign from office to avoid being indicted. His vice president, Spiro Agnew, was indicted—for extortion, tax fraud, bribery, and conspiracy. Agnew got to plead no contest on the condition that he resign from office, making him the second vice president in history to leave his position. He was the same vice president who had called me "the most dangerous man in America."

When a government abandons its founding principles, is civil disobedience an appropriate response?

---

42 Ibid.

The Sixties Movement answered that question with America's largest arrest. We were criticized for our logistics and youthful excitement, but historians described our three-stage mobilization as the event that unnerved a sitting president. White House aide Jeb Magruder said the protest had "shaken" Nixon and his staff to the core. CIA Director Richard Helms called May Day "a very damaging kind of event," noting that it was "one of the things that was putting increasing pressure on the administration to try and find some way to get out of the war." During congressionaltestimony, members of the White House staff described May Day as the event that motivated the president to end the war.

I return to this largely forgotten history because a new generation is facing a far greater challenge today. This time the stakes are even higher. Does the last generation on Earth have the right to shut the government down when gridlock rules and senators have been shackled by special interests and are unable to stand up for future generations of humanity?

Our global civilization is chained to an unsustainable engine and governments seem unable to rise to the occasion as humanity comes to the crossroads. Supported by a society that wants to believe everything is fine, no government on Earth seems able to reverse course on civilization's destructive consumption momentum. With time running out, a new generation is called to rise to the occasion and change the outcome. With humanity heading for the brink, only a global movement seems able to forge a sustainable option for how to live and thrive on Earth without destroying the planet.

We faced horrific crimes against humanity in 1971, but we face greater challenges today. That's why a new generation is called to change the world once more. With science sounding the alarm, let us draw strength from Our Roots and realize the Sixties call for massive civil disobedience may become relevant again.

Chapter 8

THE COOLING OF AMERICA

John and Yoko Memories

Leaving the crowds of D.C., I caught a ride back to Morgan's Mill Farm. I was let out into a pitch black night and walked a narrow mountain road twelve miles through an oak forest taking a long country stroll while also taking stock.

I tried to imagine what was coming next as I was greeted that night by whippoorwills and croaking male frogs. I sat on the bank of a blue gill fishing pond until exhaustion pulled me into a deep sleep. The next morning, a million blackberry petals were spread out on the water like a white magic carpet in front of me and the serenity of the morning evoked a feeling in me that "all questions are open." I felt no need to worry about what was coming next but I also never imagined that John Lennon was right around the corner.

John Lennon wanted to come out against the Vietnam War in a fashion that would be novel and dramatic—but not too serious. He and Yoko Ono cooked up an idea they called "Bed-In for Peace." They booked their first event in the Amsterdam Hilton Hotel for March 25 through 31, just before our MayDay civil disobedience when I was preoccupied and unaware of their plans. At their second Bed-In, however, I paid attention as one of the world's most prominent couples publicly declared their opposition to the Vietnam War.

Their Bed-In was planned for New York City, but got moved to the Bahamas when John's visa request was denied because of a prior cannabis conviction in England. As he realized the hot, sticky Bahamas climate would make sitting in bed for days uncomfortable, he changed his plans again. He and Yoko checked into Montreal's Queen Elizabeth Hotel on May 26, where they spent the entire week sitting in a hotel bed "like angels"

(John's words) in a public event that was part honeymoon and part antiwar protest.[43]

Tommy Sanders, Al Capp, Tim Leary, Dick Gregory, and Allen Ginsberg were invited to Montreal, and everyone but Al Capp got singing parts in Lennon's new Peace Anthem "Give Peace a Chance." Andre Perry recorded the music and guest interviews for the Canadian Broadcasting Corporation from the hotel room.

I watched John and Yoko's Bed-In for Peace on television like everyone else, thinking to myself that the Cooling of America may have just been favored by a miracle from heaven.

John and Yoko were eventually granted temporary B-2 visitors' visas to stay in the United States from August, 1971 to February, 1972. That meant they could move to New York City. John had loved New York since his first visit as a "Fab Four" Beatle. He called New York City "the cultural center of the world" like the city of Rome was the center of the world during the Roman Empire. As soon as he and Yoko moved to New York, he let it be known he wanted to be involved in the movement so Jerry Rubin and Abbie Hoffman reached out to him. When they met the first time, Lennon explained to Jerry he wanted to compose songs for the revolution, take his music on the road, and give all the money back to the people. John said he was ready to be part of a political rock 'n' roll show.[44] Jerry proposed that John consider an antiwar tour that would cross the United States and support the movement.

Lennon loved the idea of breaking free from his superstar shackles to explore more relevant music, and move away from an environment of screaming fans. James Mitchell wrote the definitive book about this phase of John Lennon's life and summed up his hopes and dreams this way: "he loved the idea that he could, more or less, freely walk around Manhattan just like everyone else."[45]

He and Yoko temporarily stayed at Midtown's St. Regis Hotel before moving into a two-room apartment at 105 Bank Street on

---

43 Mitchell, James A. *The Walrus and The Elephants, John Lennon's Years of Revolution*. New York: Seven Stories Press, 2013. p. 21.

44 Ibid.

45 Ibid.

the west side of Greenwich Village. That's where John, Yoko, and I met for the first time.

Compared to his English Tittenhurst estate with its Beatlemania trappings, this New York apartment was modest. When I walked in to meet John, he was sitting in a king-size bed in front of a giant TV screen, clicking and channel surfing just like I do.

Beatles' manager Brian Epstein had tried to exert some influence on Lennon's early dress code and attitudes on stage and while Lennon initially resisted Epstein's demands for a more professional appearance, he did eventually adjust.[46] Epstein preferred that the Beatles stay away from "controversial" positions like the Vietnam War—and he had his reasons too. When the media reported that British youth believed the Beatles were more popular than Jesus, Epstein got a firsthand experience of what public controversy feels like. Even with the majority of U.S. public opinion supporting our movement's position to withdraw GIs from Vietnam, Epstein preferred not to embroil the Beatles with hot-button media issues that might stir up more controversy. Lennon, on the other hand, saw himself as a rebel from the start. He had believed for years that the Beatles should have taken a more active part in the movement. Now with the Beatles over and done, he could be more relevant. When Mitchell interviewed me for his book about Lennon, I put it this way: "John Lennon symbolized an entire generation through the Beatles. Now he was making statements that clearly indicated he was beyond platitudes like 'I'm for peace.' This was someone saying, 'I'm an activist. I'm ready to join up'."[47] That's how it seemed to me when I first met Lennon in his NY apartment too. He completely understood the risks of joining us, but was ready to be involved and knew he could make a difference.

At our second meeting, I made Jerry's tour proposal more concrete. I suggested that John should organize the musicians, and I would organize the sponsors and speakers for each event. We would tour forty-two cities and finish up in San Diego at the Republican National Convention with a million people. Funds from each event would be shared between local organizations and the national antiwar coaltion, and each city would have one

46 http://en.wikipedia.org/wiki/File:John_Lennon_1964_001_cropped.png Epstein.

47 Mitchell, James A. The Walrus and The Elephants, John Lennon's Years of Revolution. New York: Seven Stories Press, 2013.

issue to bring public focus to our various causes over the course of the tour.

While this idea would have scared most successful entertainers trying to protect their celebrity brand, John Lennon had zero hesitation. He responded with three words: "Let's do it." That was the moment I had no doubt. All I could do was tip my hat and say to myself, "Bravo, John."

Yoko was deeply involved too. I told friends she seemed more spiritual than political. Yoko is the Japanese word for "ocean child" and Ono means "small field." At 5' 2", she would say, "It is nice to keep oneself small, like a grain of rice." Her father had been a respected banker and her education was aristocratic, but during World War II, she had to sell family possessions for food. She had experienced hardship and once told *Esquire* magazine, "Nothing is permanent."

When our movement began in the early Sixties, Yoko Ono wanted everyone to think of the word "YES" for thirty seconds and do it often. She said, one word could be a great positive affirmation filled with positive optimism. She even created an art exhibit with a tiny YES painted on a canvas displayed on a high ceiling in the Indica Gallery of London. A visitor had to climb a white ladder in the center of the room and peer through a magnifying glass hung from the ceiling to see the word written in tiny letters on the ceiling. It was that exhibit that first brought Yoko and John together. When John climbed the ladder and saw the word, he announced to the press, "It's a great relief when you get up the ladder and look through the spyglass and it doesn't say no... it says YES." When I heard what John said after climbing the ladder, I thought to myself, here is one smart man given his path to marry Yoko Ono.

One evening, John and I visited Yoko's one-person art show in Manhattan. The public had been notified that Lennon was coming to a Yoko Ono exhibit in New York City.

That meant there would be no inconspicuous stroll through Greenwich Village this night. As John and I arrived for the exhibit, only the sidewalk separated our vehicle from the exhibit side door. Nevertheless, police barricades were up and policemen stood shoulder to shoulder, forming a tunnel of protection for us to dart through. John bolted like a lightning flash out of the limo and into the museum, with me scrambling behind through the screaming pandemonium.

For viewing this compendium of Yoko's work, John had arranged reserved seats on the front row. As I sat quietly in the large room surrounded by the creative art of Yoko Ono, I had the feeling of being in coexistence with the whole world. I felt like a person who had just discovered a buried treasure called the imagination of Yoko Ono—and I knew it was special.

John and I sketched out our American tour plan and our first event was Ann Arbor, Michigan. John said he wanted a surprise unannounced guest at each venue but didn't realize a mystery guest would be coming to Ann Arbor as well. A superstar had called our Michigan producer just before the benefit to say he wanted to come too. They decided between themselves to keep it quiet since the event was sold out anyway.

Our focus in Ann Arbor was the issue of political prisoners in the United States. John wanted the first Michigan event to bring focus to the case of John Sinclair who had received a ten year sentence for possessing two marijuana joints. All his appeals were routinely denied and he had already served two and a half years.

John Sinclair was the Chairman of the Rainbow People's Party. One evening a woman wearing hippie clothes came to a public artist workshop in Detroit and asked him for a joint. He rolled one and they had a smoke. When she asked to take another with her, Sinclair rolled a second, never imagining she was a member of the Detroit Police Department. A month later, the police took their entrapment strategy to the next level and issued a warrant to arrest Sinclair. He was sentenced to the state prison in Jackson for nine-and-a-half to ten years for the possession of 11.50 grams of marijuana.

From jail, John Sinclair decided to organize a benefit rally. With the help of Michigan students, the coliseum for the University of Michigan basketball team was secured, and Peter Andrews—an experienced music promoter—was asked to organize a benefit at the Crisler Arena. Andrews felt concerned the benefit might fall short of expectations, which prompted Sinclair's wife, Leni, to speak with Jerry Rubin, who spoke with John Lennon. Lennon thought the story of John Sinclair was a good way to begin our

U.S. tour so Andrews flew to New York with Leni just to be sure this unimaginable fantasy was happening. He met John and Yoko in their West Village apartment and presented a contract for John to sign that paid the handsome sum of $500 for his appearance. John crossed out the payment and wrote in that the funds were "to be donated to the John Sinclair Freedom Fund." Later, Lennon made a cassette recording announcing that he and Yoko were coming to Michigan. With one priceless cassette, the Free John Sinclair Committee held a press conference and played it for the assembled media:

> Hello, this is John with Yoko here. I just want to say we're coming along to the John Sinclair bust fund rally to say hello. I won't be bringing a band or nothing like that because I'm only here as a tourist, but I'll probably fetch me guitar, and I know we have a song that we wrote for John Sinclair. So that's that.[48]

Following the breakup of the Beatles, a John Lennon performance had become a rather rare and special occasion. I went to Ann Arbor, somewhat dazzled by the proposition that our first Michigan rally was going to debut forty other events leading up to our culmination gathering at the Republican Party nominating convention. I saw the Ann Arbor rally as our trial balloon. Since our movement was cooling down and waning, I wanted to see how this tour would be received. When tickets went on sale and the venue sold out in forty-five minutes, I thought to myself, there will be no Cooling of America with John Lennon on board.

The entertainers who performed in Ann Arbor were John Lennon, Yoko Ono, Phil Ochs, The Up, Commander Cody and His Lost Planet Airmen, Bob Seger, Archie Shepp, Joy of Cooking, David Peel, Teegarden & Van Winkle and an unnamed artist. The speakers were John Sinclair—speaking by telephone from jail—and Bobby Seale, Jerry Rubin, Allen Ginsberg, James Groppi, Sheila Murphy, Jonnie Lee Tillmon, Ed Sanders, and me.[49]

Stevie Wonder was the surprise guest entertainer and when he walked on stage, the whole coliseum felt like a wave of rolling thunder. Stevie started by making his own statement: "Before

---

48 "The Day a Beatle Came to Town." *Ann Arbor Chronicle. December 27, 2009.*http://annarborchronicle.com/2009/12/27/the-day-a-beatle-came-to-town/
49 Ibid.

coming here today," he said, "I had a lot of things on my mind, a lot of things that you don't have to see to understand. We are in a very troublesome time today in the world. A time in which a man can get twelve years in prison for possession of marijuana, and another who can kill four students at Kent State and come out free. What kind of shit is that?"[50] He called out to the cheering crowd.

For me, the highlight of the evening was a telephone call from John Sinclair, broadcast live into the arena from prison. As John Sinclair conveyed his belief that he would soon be reunited with his wife and daughter, tearful eyes filled the hall and I was somewhat carried away by the emotional moment myself. Since I followed John Sinclair as the next speaker, I announced to the gathering that if John were not released in two weeks, we would shut down the City of Detroit. It was a bit bold but I believed it could be done. I was also relieved when it wasn't necessary.

John and Yoko (Jerry Rubin on drums)

David Fenton Photo

50 Ibid.

John and Yoko took the stage around 3 a.m. I was amazed to see that their makeshift band included Jerry Rubin, who, to my knowledge, had never publicly performed in a large gathering as a musical entertainer. Lennon also made a statement to the audience: "We came here not only to help John and to spotlight what's going on, but also to show and to say to all of you that apathy isn't it, and that we can do something. Okay, so flower power didn't work. So what? We start again."

The music of John Lennon that night spanned many movement issues, including the Attica prison uprising, women's liberation, and the freeing of John Sinclair. He even wrote a song—"It Ain't Fair, John Sinclair"—and sang it just for the occasion.

Seventy-two hours after the concert, Sinclair was freed too—well in advance of my two-week deadline. The Michigan Supreme Court granted Sinclair his release three days after the rally, overturning six previous appeals. The court order meant the state penitentiary in Jackson had to let him go. Sinclair had a tearful reunion with his wife and daughter after nearly to two and a half years of separation. I left Ann Arbor feeling hopeful that our movement had found a new beginning. For John and Yoko, Michigan was a new beginning but an end as well.

The Nixon administration was beside itself with our announcement that we would bring a million people to the Republican National Convention. When the press discovered that a lobbyist for the International Telephone and Telegraph Corporation had written a memo suggesting that ITT should pledge $400,000 for the Republican convention in return for the Justice Department setting aside its antitrust case against the company, the Republicans opted for a two-prong strategy—no public scandal of their party and no antiwar protests at their convention. Although they had secured convention facilities in San Diego, they withdrew from their contracts and moved their convention to Miami Beach, Florida, where they knew protests would be more difficult to mount. At the same time, the Justice Department came down hard on John Lennon's New York visa status.

In Jon Weiner's book, *Come Together: John Lennon in His Time,* I learned that Republican Senator Strom Thurmond—a member of the Senate Internal Security Subcommittee of the Judiciary Committee—had written a secret memorandum titled "John Lennon." Describing Lennon's appearance at the Sinclair rally and his connections with members of the Chicago Seven, the Thurmond memo stated that Lennon was part of a plan to disrupt the Republican National Convention and that "[Rennie] Davis and his cohorts intended to use John Lennon as a drawing card to promote their success... This can only inevitably lead to a clash between a controlled mob organized by this group and law enforcement officials in San Diego..." The memo concluded that if Lennon's visa was terminated, that would be a smart strategic counter-measure.[51]

With the New Year ringing in, the Nixon administration launched its "strategic countermeasure" against its public enemy number one—John Lennon. A four-year campaign to deport him back to England embroiled him in years of legal battles with immigration authorities. John and Yoko tried to stay involved with the movement as best they could by attending events like the "post-election wake" at Jerry Rubin's New York home in 1972 after McGovern's crushing defeat by Richard Nixon. But with their intensive FBI surveillance and undercover agents monitoring their every movement—and the advice of their legal team—Lennon's ability to continue the U.S. tour against the Vietnam War came to a close.

Life is mysterious. When the Nixon administration decided to push Lennon out of the United States to keep him out of our movement, he turned to immigration specialist Leon Wildes. Wildes insisted he had never heard of John Lennon until that moment. But Wildes knew how to mount brilliant legal strategies for extending Lennon's stay in the United States.

The Immigration and Naturalization Service (INS) had never previously acknowledged it used discretion when deciding who to deport. Through the Freedom of Information Act, Wildes discovered there were 1,843 cases when the INS used prosecutorial discretion in the past. When this secret program was discovered and the story broke in the media, the INS had to concede its use of discretion in "non-priority" cases. Because of the Lennon case, new guidelines were issued about non-priority discretion. Lennon eventually won his case by obtaining a "non-priority" classification himself. In doing so, he also created a precedent that President Barack Obama was able to draw upon as

---

51 Glenn, Alan. "The Day a Beatle Came to Town." *The Ann Arbor Chronicle*. December 27, 2009. Also, Wiener, John. *Come Together: John Lennon In His Time*. Urbana-Champaign, IL: U of Illinois P, 1990.

a new legal authority four decades later. The Lennon case became the legal foundation for the Obama administration's decision to defer the deportation of more than 580,000 immigrants who had been brought into the country as children. Obama's legal authority drew from the Lennon precedent. In fact, it was pivotal to the White House deliberations over what could be legally done for American immigrants without congressional action. When the AP story of the Obama administration's program was published, Wildes declared that John Lennon must be smiling in his grave.[52]

With the shutting down of the Lennon antiwar tour, the Cooling of America fully set in, dampening the fire of the 1960s like the chill of a harsh winter. As the Sixties Movement wound down, I decided to support a small demonstration at the Republican Convention in Miami Beach. I stopped eating and did a water fast, as part of the protest. Dick Gregory, a comedian who was active in the movement and a friend, flew to Miami Beach to coach me on how to do it safely.

For forty-two days in the tropical climate of Miami Beach, I fasted as I watched cumulus clouds forming at low altitudes expand into giant cumulonimbus pink color radiations when the sun went down. All my senses were heightened as those pink clouds reminded me of that classic song of psychedelia, "Lucy in the Sky with Diamonds." With my senses heightened from the fast, every sight and sound astounded me as though I was in a dreamy magical realm that was not uncomfortable but unexpected.

I appreciated everyone I met when I was fasting, especially our Miami Beach fan club—the hundreds of sweet senior residents who kept telling me I reminded them of their son. They turned out in droves when I spoke to any neighborhood organization. They praised our dwindling movement and kept telling me not to feel discouraged because we were still the cat's meow.

On the day of the presidential nomination, I was in the front of a march heading toward the Republican convention hall when we were rudely halted with canisters of tear gas launched as flying projectiles. The first canister exploded against my chest. Since it was day forty-two of my fast, it was not a good day for toxic gas

52 Associated Press. "Obama Immigration Policy Rooted in John Lennon Deportation Case." September 4, 2014. http://www.billboard.com/articles/business/6243643/obama-immigrationpolicy-john-lennon-deportation-case

overload. Dazed, sick, and unable to walk, I got a little help from my friends, who carried me to a nearby apartment where I spent a long night teetering. Miami Beach seniors, however, never backed down when facing that tear gas. They were fearless as they brought their buckets of water and face cloths to our aid and hustled our gas afflicted demonstrators into their homes like grandmothers protect their grandchildren.

Richard Nixon was nominated and easily won the election. His campaign emphasized his "success" in "nearly ending" the Vietnam war and opening diplomatic relations with China. The only President later forced to resign from office due to scandal, he won by a wider popular margin than any previous U.S. President. With Nixon's nomination secured in Miami Beach and my fast broken with a canister of tear gas, I was starting to feel like one of those advertisements for migraine headaches.

Since my parents retired on the west side of Florida, I went to their home after the Republican convention and borrowed their motorboat to head into the Gulf of Mexico for a week on a deserted island. I walked the uninhabited beaches and swam under tropical trees that were home for thousands of birds. My senses were still acute and alive from the water fast so this beautiful island seemed super vibrant to me. I felt a transition beginning. It felt like a slow boat to China. With dedicated years to a movement to change the world, I was going back to society but would not be rushed. I was not alone in my slow pace either.

As the Sixties movement wound down, tens of thousands of activists took their sweet time traveling the oceans, lakes, islands, mountains and fields of nature as they made their way back to careers, marriages, and families. On the way back to "normal," many of us lived in tents, log cabins, and farmhouses. We grew our own crops, hauled water from wells, discovered medicinal plants for natural cures, and learned basic survival skills. We experienced a brief training in self-sufficiency and the intelligence of nature— skills that will be valuable in the time that is coming.

As we returned to society and took up careers, some of us realized we had a spiritual side too.

I made plans with Allen Ginsberg to spend a year alone in the Sierra Mountains on his remote and beautiful property—just to be quiet—but my plans changed when I was invited by Madam Nguyen Thi Binh to attend the Paris ceremonies that formalized the U.S.-Vietnam Peace Accord.

On my flight to Paris, I met Larry Canada, a former roommate who was headed for India and had plans to visit some of their sacred sites. He urged me to join him. Following the footsteps of the Beatles and thousands of others, I decided to go. It was a decision that mirrored a growing Western curiosity with meditation and Eastern traditions. Lennon's interest in India was an example and George Harrison also opened a door to India with his sitar lessons from Ravi Shankar. Before the Chicago Democratic Convention, the Beatles attended a Transcendental Meditation training at the ashram of Maharishi Mahesh Yogi. When I visited India for the first time, I learned a meditation I still practice today.

As the Sixties Movement wound down, my new interest in meditation seemed shocking to some of political friends. Eldridge Cleaver was a prominent leader in the Black Panther Party who had decided to embrace Christianity to the upset of his friends too. Looking back on this time, trips to India and adventures into nature seemed to spur a type of 'quiet revolution' that over the decades grew into yoga, self-evaluation, checking egos and other practices that were not that common to previous political movements. .

In today's movement, we can already see that large protest mobilizations are stronger than ever. Defending America's core values has broad public appeal and can succeed if we stay nonviolent. But realize that another part of our movement has its roots in that "quiet revolution" that began as the Sixties came to an end. The new humanity movement is organizing empowered communities where people can live and thrive. Once food insecurity sets in and cities realize they need to create a new way of living themselves, our new-living networks will seem important to an unsustainable humanity in trouble.

Gandhi's adage to be the change that changes the world will seem self-evident to New Humanity communities that know how to live and thrive. Today's movement ignited by Donald J. Trump will stand up for humanity. But a new segment of our movement whose roots began towards the end of the Sixites will become a welcomed addition as we grow and evolve.

Building a global movement also requires that each and every one of us align ourselves with one or more of our three natural affinities:

1. **Our reform movement** is non-violently resisting entrenched institutions and hard right executive orders by focusing on Congressional advocacy and electoral politics. As climate change knocks on our own doors, our reform segment will spread to businesses, neighborhoods and work places to create Earth-friendly towns, regenerative livelihoods and conscious, sustainable businesses.

2. **Our political revolution movement** is standing up for humanity by powerfully pushing back on every hard right effort to register or deport Muslims, privatize the general welfare, develop Artic drilling, build dangerous crude oil pipelines, pull out of the Paris Climate agreement, dismantle the UN, remove pubic protections of wilderness sanctuaries, deport dreamers, roll back public health care, restrict voting rights, repress racial and gender equality and gut the mission of the EPA. The political revolution movement includes our non-violent civil disobedient champions whose courage has no bounds.

3. **Our New Humanity movement** appreciates the need to change ourselves—to be the change the changes the world. The New Humanity is supported by a "quiet revolution" that includes a worldwide Permaculture network, breakthrough technologies, Earth Whisperers, a global spiritual family and sustainable, self-sufficiency advocates advancing whole system solutions aligned with the intelligence of nature. As one segment of our movement powerfully stands up for humanity, another must quietly build sustainable new-living communities that have no requirement to solve problems by pointing the finger. Pioneering a new human awareness, the New Humanity understands that what we fear is what we attract. Advancing the proposition that we can change the outcome out of a great turning in ourselves, the New Humanity is pioneering a new nation on Earth from a journey to evolve.

We have different approaches to changing the world but if we respect our differences and do not turn on each other, we can change the world together again.

The Sixties was a generation that did not settle down in suburban houses like our parents thought we should. We didn't get trapped by the financial constrictions of our parents. Instead, we set out to change the world. While we initially walked by each other without seeing who we were before we ignited, we came out of hiding to change the world. A similar phenomenon is happening again. Today's movement is designing a nation that can change the world.

Abbie Hoffman once said during the Chicago Seven trial that the Sixties Movement was a nation whose address was our own state of mind. Today is similar. As we unlock our full measure of passion and realize our movement is larger than the American Revolution, the Sixties Revolution and the Renaissance combined, coming events will support us to forge a nation that changes the human condition. Some activists may want to stay consumed with their anger but a vast segment of humanity yearns to pioneer a new way of living in every facet of life—spirituality and awareness, education and discovery, currency and barter, building and construction, health and wellness, organizational best practices, free power generation, land regeneration, Earth travel, space travel, a new economic model that respects life on Earth, a new role for chemicals, new manufacturing standards and new systems for data, information, and privacy. Only a nation can contain the vision to write a new human story. Only a new generation can underwrite a new human stewardship with animals, insects, plants, and the Earth. We can accomplish the task that is great if we stay in our beauty and remain unfettered by how it was done in the past.

When it comes time for the New Humanity to choose its philosophy, we should first realize what we are not.

We are not a new Utopia based on a new theory of everything. The "Invisible Hand" where negative egos go unchecked as the best philosophy for promoting "the common good" is not our economic axiom. We have no need to promote discredited systems like communism to end the evils of capitalism either. Individual ownership with the right to maximize one's personal fortune without regard to the consequences to life on Earth is not our Promised Land. Private ownership may work when profits are appropriately shared and the business purpose supports positive, sustainable outcomes aligned with the intelligence of nature, but private ownership that causes the destruction of the middle class, the promotion of bigoted divides, the extreme stratification of wealth, and the subordination of the many by the few is not a philosophy for a new nation on Earth. We need a segment of our movement to actually experience a new stage of awareness where egos are checked and universal life principles emerge to support a new-living covenant.

The New Humanity understands we must heal as a species—starting with ourselves.

Can we also envision a new way of living that inspires and supports a new human being? Today's movement will defend humanity's core values from the fear and divide of the Trump effect but is that enough? We can also showcase a new way of living that supports any community struggling to cope to live and thrive without destroying the planet. Coming events will turn public attention our way if we will remember the vision of Vietnam—to set up and get ready now before the storms arrives.

The science that is sounding the alarm and the extraordinary projects currently underway are set forth in Volumes II and III of this trilogy.

How should we advance the message of the new humanity? When John Lennon performed in Ann Arbor for the John Sinclair rally, I appreciated again how large gatherings are one of the many answers. Exhilarating musical productions involving youth musicians, guest celebrities, legendary speakers, and youth leaders can spread a vision and build a movement. In the present time, a New Humanity World Tour can spread our message while solving some of humanity's biggest problems—like returning the quality of life to millions of victims of Agent Orange in Indochina and supporting sanctuary cities that defend the American dream. If we want to create an avalanche of people that can change the world, Live Earth musical performances, breakthrough technologies and a movement passionate to change ourselves will find inspiration in one of John Lennon's songs—the one that reminds us of who we are and why we are here.

Remember "Instant Karma"? His words seem more appropriate today than ever before.

> And we all shine on
> Like the moon and the stars and the sun
> Well, we all shine on
> Everyone, c'mon
>
> Instant Karma's gonna get you
> Gonna knock you off your feet
> Better recognize your brothers
> Everyone you meet
>
> Why in the world are we here?
> Surely not to live in pain and fear
> Why on Earth are you there
> When you're everywhere
> Gonna get your share
>
> Well, we all shine on
> Like the moon and the stars and the sun
> Yeah, we all shine on
> C'mon and on and on, on, on.[53]

53 Reprinted with permission from Downtown Music Publishing.

GENERATION
Arise

ABOUT THE AUTHOR

Rennie Davis was the coordinator of the largest coalition of anti-war and civil rights organizations in the late 1960s. During America's most dramatic protest events, he stood at the eye of a storm during the Chicago Democratic Convention watched on television by more people than watched the first moon landing. He was one of the Chicago Seven, described by *The New York Times* as "the most significant political trial in U.S. history." He traveled to Vietnam to return American POWs to their families. He partnered with John Lennon to bring a million people to the Republican National Convention. The Vice President of the United States called him "the most dangerous man in America."

When *Time Magazine* declared the Sixties Movement was over in one of its cover stories, Rennie Davis called for the largest civil disobedience arrest in American history. Joined by a younger John Kerry and hundreds of Vietnam veterans who returned their medals won in Vietnam to Congress, 100,000 people heard the call to stop the war with civil disobedience. A Washington, D.C. football stadium was converted into a temporary prison in an event described by historians as the decisive moment causing a U.S. President to realize he had to end the Vietnam War.

Rennie Davis is a respected spokesman of his generation and has appeared on NBC, ABC, CNN, MTV, the CBS Legend Series,

Larry King Live, Barbara Walters, the BBC, and other national media forums. Today, he supports a new generation dedicated to igniting a global movement. His roadmap for changing the world is set forth in *The New Humanity* trilogy—a movement to change the world.

THE TRILOGY

Volume I: Our Roots

Volume II: Humanity at the Crossroads

Volume III: The Rise of Ilian

THE NEW HUMANITY

A Movement to Change the World

Who are we? We are scientists, university teachers, college students, spiritual leaders, environmentalists, observant farmers, principled entrepreneurs, independent journalists, artists, free spirits, mothers concerned for their future and sages honoring the Earth. We are aligning with millions of activists in Generation Z, Millennials and Boomers. We are tens of millions of people who can see with our own eyes the accelerating global social tsunami. We understand sea levels rising mean harsh lessons are coming. We understand the rise and fall of great civilizations has happened before. We understand the greatest extinction of species since the end of the dinosaurs is occurring at the present time. We can see for ourselves that opioid addiction is the new leading cause of death in the United States—and that global terrorism, mass migrations and eco-system collapse are real-life tragedies enveloping our world. Rather than solve these critical problems, civilization is ignoring these critical problems—a denial that is fostering fear and divide and hard right movements around the world.

In a time like no other, we bear witness to an emerging modern absurdity: Republicans for Putin; fake news replacing real news; and Donald J. Trump, the President of the United States. As Greenland melts away, the New Humanity recognizes that no government on Earth seems able to mobilize an effective course correction. The United States previously played a global leadership role but America is losing its mantle as the whole world watches a Republican President abandon the vision of the United States of America.

Pure and simple, humanity is in trouble. Our oceans are dying. Our rain forests are in peril. Species extinction has jumped 10,000 times higher than the normal rate over the previous 65 million years. Recognizing the global peril, the New Humanity draws from its Roots to forge a movement to stand up for humanity again—and pioneer a new way of living on Earth today. We are the movement that changes the outcome and builds a nation that shall not perish from the Earth.

Add contact information at bottom of this section: Contact Rennie Davis at rennie@renniedavis.com; Learn more at www.ffh.org; and www.newhumanitybook.com

PHILANTHROPY

With the purchase of your book
You support

- The national effort to build support services and infrastructure for today's movement
- A Social Media Platform of bloggers, iPod outlets, internet channels and traditional media outlets that can deliver the news and inspiration of organizers, movement leaders and networks
- A New Humanity World Tour that is preparing large entertainment and message rallies to support our diverse movement causes
- Sacred Water Projects threatened by oil, chemical, agriculture and other industries (To understand the water crisis, see the movie *Last Call at the Oasis*.)
- Water Protectors for the Sioux Tribe
- On-line training for organizers and volunteers who join one of the three movement segments
- Sanctuary states that protect the American dream
- New Humanity Speaker's Bureau supporting speakers and troubadours inspiring the movement

BRING RENNIE DAVIS TO YOUR ORGANIZATION

An evening with Rennie Davis may start out exploring the proposition that civilization is unsustainable and climate change is the tip of the iceberg but Rennie is not about doom and gloom. He is about inspiring the one segment of humanity that can change the outcome. He believes a movement to change the world is the story of our time and a new generation can change the world.

Rennie Davis coordinated the largest anti-war and civil rights coalition in the 1960s. He was one of the legends of the Chicago Seven. He organized the largest civil disobedience arrest in American history and partnered with John Lennon to tour the country to end the Vietnam war. Today, he supports Millennials and Boomers, scientists and environmental leaders, personal growth and spiritual seekers, technology innovators, Black Lives Matter activists, DREAMers, and women whose shared common mission is a movement to change the world.

Praise for The New Humanity

"This book returns to my dad's time. He was Jerry Rubin. This is the story of how the Sixties happened and how a new generation can make it happen again.

— Adams Rubin
Son of Jerry Rubin

"We grew up hearing these riveting stories. By the time we were in college, we know they were important too. Many people understand humanity is in trouble but this book is for the person who wants to do something about it."

— Maya and Sky Davis
Daughter and son of Rennie Davis

More Praise for the New Humanity Message...

"Rennie Davis is a modern day Socrates. In Plato's Apology, Socrates states: 'To put it bluntly, I've been assigned to this city as if to a large horse which is inclined to be lazy and is in need of some great stinging fly and all day long I'll never cease to settle here, there, everywhere, rousing and reproving every one of you.' Rennie Davis continues to be that voice in America. His message is inspiring, optimistic, and accessible to people across a wide belief spectrum."

— Craig Angus

"Rennie is beyond the 'New.' He is 'The Next.' His heart's wisdom is where our planet should be heading.

— Rev. Lawrence Katz

Made in the USA
Monee, IL
25 October 2020